Moving int

Other titles from
Centre for Strategy and Communication

How to become a brilliant presenter
Tess Woodcraft

Taking and writing minutes
Jan Burnell

Moving into management

Julia Braggins

Centre for Strategy and Communication

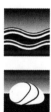

Centre for Strategy and Communication
Centre for Strategy and Communication is a centre for reflection and change.

We help individuals and organisations in the public and non profit sectors transform the way they communicate as managers.

We are committed to management which encompasses the values of public service and diversity, and places a premium on emotional intelligence and empowerment.

If you would like more information about the Centre's consultancy and training you can find our website on www.the-centre.co.uk Or contact us on 020 7490 3030

First published 2004 by
Centre for Strategy and Communication
140 Old Street, London EC1V 9BW

ISBN 0–9546315–0–1

Cartoons: Mike Turner

Produced for the Centre for Strategy and Communication by
Chase Publishing Services, Fortescue, Sidmouth, EX10 9QG
Printed in the European Union

Contents

Acknowledgements

Thanks go to all my friends and colleagues at the Centre for Strategy and Communication, from whom I have learned so much.

Like all trainers, I have been a career magpie. Ideas, checklists and materials developed by others within CSC appear below, without individual acknowledgements. Where I have drawn significantly on the work of other trainers, writers and consultants I have tried to acknowledge as much in the text. If I have inadvertently internalised your words or ideas, and have not acknowledged my debts, I apologise in advance.

Julia Braggins

1
On becoming a manager

Congratulations! You've got the job

When you become a manager everything changes. You are accountable not just for your own work, but for the work of other people too.

You have probably gained that promotion by being very good at what you do. But for the first time, you can't do it all yourself any more. In fact you will now have far less time to 'do it' at all.

Your task now is to 'get the job done through other people'. Good people skills are the number one requirement for a manager.

There are some basic management procedures that it is probably wise to follow, and certainly some helpful tips and techniques that you can learn. But 'how to manage' can't be boiled down to a set of rules and regulations.

Being a good manager is, as much as anything, a matter of how you see things, what your fundamental beliefs are, how you manage yourself, and how you are with other people.

If you are promoted from within

A lot will depend on how you gained this promotion. Were you promoted from within? In which case you have to deal with becoming one of 'them' as opposed to one of 'us'.

- You may have to defend decisions from on high with which you privately find it hard to agree
- You may have to supervise people older, and longer-serving, than you
- You may have to manage old friends. You may have to decide whether the girls' night out at the pub is still on, and if so, how you will handle it when the group starts to talk shop, to gossip or moan
- You will inevitably feel some sense of loss, as well as opportunity

Or are you brand new to the organisation?

- Again, you may be younger than some of your new supervisees and, in their eyes, less experienced
- They will inevitably know far more about the work of the organisation than you do, and yet you are supposed to be 'in charge'
- You may privately feel that the organisation is in a mess, and be tempted to refer back regularly to 'the way we did it in my last job'
- Perhaps no one has thought ahead about your arrival, or arranged any induction programme for you, so you have to find it all out as you go along
- You may (rightly or wrongly) sense hostility from your new colleagues (were any of them internal candidates for your post?)
- The anxiety provoked by new surroundings and new responsibilities can be stressful, in itself

So there's no 'best position'. But don't forget: you applied for the job because you thought you could do it, and you got it because other people were convinced that you were the best candidate. You were the one they chose. People want you to succeed!

As you read through the book, you will find a series of case studies. These are all anonymised, with details changed to preserve confidentiality, but are based on real dilemmas faced by real people. After each, I have included some possible ways forward. I want to emphasise that there are no 'right answers' – solutions which will always work, for all individuals in all circumstances. It would take a novel to sketch in all the relevant background, in each case. The options are suggested as food for thought. Try a few: see what works for you, and discard what doesn't.

Case study

Annie has worked for her organisation for 18 months. She was recruited as membership assistant by Jim, who is considerably older than her, and works part time. She was promoted to the same level as Jim after a year in the job. They get on well.

Annie's boss has recently moved on. Before her move was public knowledge, she encouraged Annie to apply for the manager's position. Although she worried about what Jim would think, Annie decided to go ahead.

When Jim learned of Annie's application, he reacted badly. However he did not apply for the post himself. The recruitment and selection process went ahead according to the book, and Annie got the job, against some outside competition.

How should Annie behave with Jim, now that she is his new manager?

Some options Annie might consider:

- Ask her new manager for support in bedding in the new team.
- Have a private word with Jim, and ask him how he feels about the situation.
- Listen carefully to his response.
- Agree with Jim, as far as possible, his own self contained work areas.
- Manage Jim with the 'lightest touch' possible, consistent with her new responsibilities.

There are no hard and fast rules: you can probably think of plenty of other good suggestions. The main things are to retain confidence, listen carefully and resist 'oversteering'. Annie got the job, after all.

2
The manager's role

So what do managers do?

If you work for a well organised employer, you will have a job description that gives a reasonable description of your new role. (NB: now you are a manager, you must make sure all your staff have one of these too, and that it is up to date!)

More than just 'the work'

But once you are a manager, you have to do a great deal more than just 'the work'. Now you will probably have to:

- Manage the people who do the work
  - recruit and select individuals
  - induct, supervise, support, develop and appraise individuals
  - give constructive feedback to team and individuals
  - delegate appropriately
  - develop an effective team
- Manage the work
  - set objectives and create action plans with the team
  - plan projects and work flows
  - bring projects in to budget and to deadline
  - manage quality of service
- Manage information and communication
  - make sure everyone has the information they need
  - make sure lines of communication are clear
  - create effective working relationships across the organisation on behalf of your team

- Manage resources
  - manage the budget for your team
  - manage equipment and space
  - manage the human resources
  - make recommendations for expenditure where necessary

Acting as an ambassador

You will probably also have to manage external relations too: you may need to liaise with:

- service users
- customers
- the local authority
- national government and government departments
- funders
- members
- peer organisations
- suppliers
- trustees and directors

and of course

- the general public

You may be asked to give presentations, you may have to handle letters of complaint, you may be asked to represent the organisation at meetings, conferences and events. You will be an ambassador for the organisation, much more obviously than before.

And as well as all this you will still probably have to do some of 'the work'!

The manager in the public and voluntary sectors

There are good and bad managers in all organisations. What characterises public and voluntary sector work is that it is not for profit.

A key characteristic of any not-for-profit sector organisation is that it is likely to have a strong value base. People who work in the organisation may care passionately about what they do, and the needs of their clients, users and beneficiaries.

'Typical' not-for-profit sector management issues, whether the organisation has five staff or 5,000, include:

- confusion about the role of board members/councillors etc. and the interface with staff
- a 'long hours' culture
- a propensity to stress and burnout
- difficulties with long term planning and goal setting
- unclear decision making and management structures
- unwillingness to recognise or deal with conflict
- unclear expectations of staff
- shortage of funds and periodic funding crises
- a related difficulty with business planning
- inadequate systems (administrative and technological)

A recent survey into bullying and harassment at work found (worryingly) that despite the assumption amongst many that people who work in the sector are 'carers', voluntary sector workers were amongst those who felt most frequently bullied by their managers.

What makes a good manager?

Think of managers you have worked with before. If you have had a good one, you have been fortunate, as you have an idea how helpful a decent manager can be. What did you most admire about the way they worked?

According to many new managers, who themselves have been managed by others in the past, a good manager:

- Knows the work
- Is consistent
- Plans ahead
- Takes decisions
- Is realistic about what can get done in a day
- Shares information

Case study

Rupal's manager constantly interferes. The team works in an open plan office, so her manager, Irene, can hear everything that's going on.

Rupal has recently become responsible for the work of two assistants, for whom Irene used to be the line manager. Irene is very ready to jump in whenever one of them takes what she considers a 'difficult' phone call, short-circuiting the line of accountability to Rupal, and frequently contradicting agreed strategies within the new team.

How can Rupal manage the situation, in order to create clarity for herself and her staff, without giving offence?

Some options Rupal might consider:

- Have a private word with Irene, preferably as soon as possible after such an incident.

- Come prepared with evidence about recent episodes, to show this was not just a 'one-off'.

- Ask Irene whether she was aware this was happening, what her major concerns were, and how Rupal could address these.

- Problem-solve with Irene to agree ways forward.

- Knows I have a life outside work – and has one too
- Recognises good work: gives praise and thanks people
- Gives constructive feedback – positive, not just negative
- Makes time for me: meets regularly with me
- Consults me regularly: involves me in decisions
- Respects me as a colleague
- Is a good listener
- Cares about me as a person
- Invests in my training and development
- Inspires trust
- Is fair: has no favourites
- Is good at boundaries
- Keeps confidences
- Never loses their temper

- Is well organised and a good time keeper
- Is loyal: supports me in public – asks questions in private

No doubt your own experience will lead you to think of other virtues, if you have been lucky enough to have had a good role model. If you have been less lucky, no doubt you can think of plenty of examples of how not to do it, from the reverse side of the coin!

Management and leadership

My boss, my manager – we tend to use these words interchangeably. But what about *my leader*? Not a phrase you hear much at work – though you might hear people talking about their *team leader*. You hear plenty about management skills, and leadership skills, however, and often in the same breath. But what are these two groups of skills? Are they similar, overlapping, or just different?

- 'Lead', at its root, means 'go, travel, guide'. We want our leaders to go first on the journey.
- The root origin of 'manage' is *'manus'* (Latin for 'hand'). 'The safe pair of hands'. Managing is about organisation and control. The manager need not be a visionary.
- 'The leader does the right thing. The manager does things right.'
- But leaders without management skills can become dictators. Managers without leadership skills will never inspire their teams. Ideally you need strengths on both sides.

What we want in our leaders

The Industrial Society (now renamed the Work Foundation) did some research a few years ago into what 1,000 people rated important in a leader. Here are the top 20 behaviours, in rank order. According to this study the good leader:

1. shows enthusiasm
2. supports other people
3. recognises individual effort
4. listens to individuals' ideas and problems

5. provides direction
6. demonstrates personal integrity
7. practises what they preach
8. encourages teamwork
9. actively encourages feedback
10. develops other people
11. promotes other people's self esteem
12. seeks to understand before making judgements
13. treats mistakes as learning opportunities
14. gives people doing the work the power to make decisions
15. encourages new ways of doing things
16. promotes understanding of the key issues
17. looks at possible future challenges
18. agrees targets
19. takes decisions
20. minimises anxiety

It looks as though it is the people skills that differentiate the leader from the manager. But it takes more than good people skills to be a good leader.

The Industrial Society study found that we want leaders with the right fundamental beliefs. We want leaders with:

- self belief
- integrity and fairness, and
- a belief in others

Self belief

If you, as leader, come across regularly as defensive, apologetic, or unsure of yourself, staff may feel they have to reassure you. This can make them feel resentful: after all, it's your job to reassure and bolster them. They are also reluctant to follow someone who does not appear to know where they are going.

'Don't promote your weaknesses: you won't be promoted for them.'

Integrity and fairness

If you, as leader, have favourites, treat people differently on irrelevant grounds, break confidences, or operate double standards of any kind, this will be bitterly resented. If you do not have, and maintain, high standards of personal and professional conduct, it is likely that colleagues will find you out.

It is best to work on the assumption that your every decision and deed is transparent to all. Although it is not appropriate to broadcast everything, you should be acting in such a way that, if news of any decision or practice were to leak out, there is nothing of which you would feel ashamed. Your values and actions will be far more visible than you think, anyway!

A belief in others

As Sir John Harvey Jones, management and television guru, said:

> *'Leadership is about getting extraordinary results from ordinary people.'*

I have always worked best for managers who seemed to see in me more than I saw in myself, and who encouraged me. Such leaders inspire us to heights of which we did not believe ourselves capable.

We want to be able to trust our leaders. It's an added bonus if we like them. But only if we can admire and respect them will they inspire us to give of our best.

> *'As for the best leaders, the people do not notice their existence. The next best, the people honour and praise. The next, the people fear; and the next the people hate. When the best leaders' work is done, the people say, "We did it ourselves".'* (Lao-Tsu)

Case study

John has taken up his first chief executive post in a small, ailing charity. The chair of trustees, Mark, was seriously ill when John arrived. He did not give John any induction, appearing to think only of the task of keeping the agency afloat. John's first few meetings with Mark were difficult.

John spent his first few months feeling unsupported, anxious and angry. He wondered whether to resign. After much heart searching, he decided to stay on and see if he could make a go of it.

In the autumn, Mark died. How should John move forward?

Some options John might consider:

- Work towards the appointment of a new chair of trustees, with whom he can get on. John needs someone with management experience, who knows how to listen.

- Agree a game plan for working in partnership. The relationship between the chair and the chief executive is key to the successful functioning of the charity.

- If there is no strategic planning process in operation, think through ways to begin one. It sounds as though this charity has lost its way, and needs to go back to square one. What is its primary task? What objectives should it be setting itself, and how can it plan to meet them? An away day with an external facilitator might help. That way, John and the new chair could contribute too.

- John may need to find some external support for himself. Non-managerial supervision can be extremely valuable, in lonely jobs like these, and is well worth considering. This would provide John with a confidential space to explore his options and think through realistic strategies for managing himself in the role.

3
Managing the task
and planning ahead

'The nicest thing about not planning is that failure comes as a complete surprise and is not preceded by a period of worry and depression'. (Anon.)

When you move into management, you are no longer just responsible for your own work. You will have to manage other people's work as well as your own, and you will have to manage projects. This calls for some thought about planning.

How organised is your organisation?

Do you have a strategic plan? It may be called:

- a development plan, or
- a business plan, or
- something else

It will be about the direction the organisation is taking, typically over the next three to five years.

A central purpose for the plan is to make the case for the organisation.

What matters is the planning process, rather than the resulting document. All involved with the organisation need to feel some ownership of the plan.

Starting from scratch is hard. The organisation needs to consult everyone involved: trustees/directors, members, staff, volunteers, beneficiaries, funders, and everyone with a stake in the organisation. This will usually result in a plan with something like the following elements:

- Vision (the world we want to see)
- Mission (what we have to do to bring that about)
- Objectives (how we propose to do it)

This will lead to an action plan, perhaps for the year, which will identify specific goals under each of the objectives. These will drive performance across the organisation, through teams to individuals.

A good plan will be used regularly, like a map, not put away with relief once the planning meetings are over. It's helpful to review the whole thing, including the 'big picture' statements (vision, mission or statements of purpose, or whatever you call them) once every five years or so.

The fine tuning will need more regular attention. Many organisations have an annual planning process: the 'big' objectives will yield annual goals, which need review and evaluation.

But nothing stands still. Ideally, your planning process will allow for both **Focus** and **Flexibility**.

Where are you going?

All organisations are going in one direction or another – even if it is only over the cliff and into the sea. In poorly managed organisations you will see a lot of effort wasted, because individual efforts are not coordinated. Some people seem to be going at right angles to others, or sideways, or even backwards.

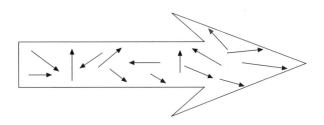

You can see that, if the figure above were a shark, it wouldn't swim very well!

The strong organisation has thought about where it is going, and has ensured that all those involved in it are putting their efforts into pulling in the same direction. It has strategic goals, and the different individuals, teams and departments have their differing roles to play, in the effort to deliver achievements against those goals.

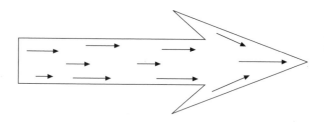

The shark above looks as though it would cut through the water a lot more effectively.

Goals and targets

There is no point in having spent the effort on devising a strategic plan if you cannot see how you are doing in terms of the goals you have set. Your organisation will probably have set timed and measurable targets for each team and department, and you will have the task of meeting some of these, with the help of your team. So you are going to have to think about how you do this.

Target setting requires real clarity about what to measure and how to measure it. On the one hand, 'what gets measured gets managed'. On the other hand, some of the most important outcomes are notoriously hard to measure, in any meaningful way.

" I SEE YOU MANAGING FAR BETTER
EMPLOYING A STRATEGIC ACTION PLAN
RATHER THAN A CRYSTAL BALL ! "

Case study

Jeremy is a project manager in a young organisation working with rough sleepers. It has only been going for six years, and has grown at a fast pace. New projects have mushroomed as funding has become available. The organisation is run by its charismatic founder, who 'does not believe in business plans'.

Jeremy wants to set up a volunteering scheme, across the organisation's six projects. He feels this would have many benefits, and is needed urgently, to cope with increasing demand.

However, there is a history of bad experiences in using volunteers in two of the projects – for very different reasons. They are blocking progress. Jeremy needs everyone to buy in to the scheme for it to work, but there is no mechanism for agreeing a shared way forward.

How might Jeremy move things on?

Some options Jeremy might consider:

- Seek support from his own manager. If this is the chief executive, so much the better. If not, his manager needs to be persuaded first that this scheme would have real advantages for the organisation. The effort to do this might help Jeremy to think through the case afresh. Is he still sure it's a good idea, himself?

- He might offer to do a paper for the senior management team on the use of volunteers, perhaps highlighting the successes of other comparable organisations in the field.

- Jeremy might want to start his researches by seeking guidance from an organisation like the National Centre for Volunteering, which could save him reinventing the wheel.

- As well as stressing the benefits, Jeremy needs to cost out any proposals carefully. He should include costs which are sometimes hidden, like the cost of policy development, the additional management charges to supervise the volunteers properly, administration and staff training, as well as the more obvious things like volunteer recruitment and expenses.

- Without any kind of an organisation-wide plan, Jeremy may find it harder to show how the volunteers will contribute to achieving the organisation's objectives than he would have done otherwise. Perhaps he could gently argue for the value of some kind of strategic planning exercise across the organisation as a whole – but call it something different. Maybe if he suggested a six year review, this might lead naturally into a systematic look at the bigger picture. Often, changing the language helps.

For instance, say a school wants to measure the extent to which it is succeeding in producing active citizens. How would it select its measures?

- Numbers of pupils involved in voluntary activity in the community?
- Numbers of pupils with practical experience of the way local government works?
- Numbers of pupils with a testable understanding of the way national government works?

Or are 'numbers of pupils' not the right thing to be counting? After all, what we want to know is: what difference have we made? Not just: How many pupils have taken part in our programme?

It is easy to become cynical, and give up the search for sensible measures. 'Bean-counting' is often dismissed. However, we still need to work out sensible ways of checking whether or not we are adding value.

SMARTER targets

SMART is a time-honoured management acronym. It stands for:

- **S**pecific
- **M**easurable
- **A**chievable and agreed
- **R**elevant and realistic
- **T**ime related

We need to make sure that all our goals and targets, whether for ourselves or those we manage, are SMART.

For instance, I may want to increase the membership of our society. First I need to think:

- **Specific**: do I want to increase all members, or shall I focus on a sub-group – solicitors? women with children under five? Council tax payers in Solihull? What and who?

Then my target needs to be:

- **Measurable**: I won't know if I've succeeded if I don't give myself a figure to aim at. For instance I could aim to increase membership **by 5%**.

- **Achievable and agreed**: my target must be **achievable**. Perhaps I've just got far too much on. Perhaps the market is saturated. And I won't sign up to delivering on any target if I haven't **agreed** it.

- **Relevant and realistic**: it must be **relevant**, both to my job role (perhaps I'm nothing to do with the membership: perhaps I'm the office manager) and to the organisation, otherwise I might feel this wasn't a **relevant** target for me. Similarly, if we've already held a big marketing drive to get people to pay by direct debit over the last six months, perhaps a commitment to increasing payment by direct debit by a further 5% isn't **realistic** just at the moment.

- **Time related**: I must know **by when** I've got to achieve this 5% increase. 5% over the next year might be feasible, whilst 5% over the next quarter might be a tall order. Similarly (relating back to the **realistic** above) I must have the spare capacity. If I've already got difficulties fitting everything into the working day, then I'll have to start being assertive with my manager!

To these we could add:

- Evaluated, and
- Reviewed

to get SMARTER.

We always need to evaluate and review. It is always important to check that these targets are still the right ones, and keep tabs on their value for us as we go along.

And at the end of the time period (or at appraisal, when this sort of target setting exercise might most obviously come up) manager and staff member need to do a review.

- How did we get on?
- If it didn't work out, why not? What could we have done differently? What has changed, elsewhere? What can we learn for the future?
- Celebrate success! (NB: always do your best to set targets as conservatively as is consonant with the needs of the organisation. That way, everyone can enjoy the buzz that successful delivery brings).

Case study

Nadia has just been promoted to her first team leader's job in a housing project for people with learning difficulties. She came from a similar organisation, but this is a new team for her. Staff have to sleep in, and there is regular difficulty in covering the weekend and bank holiday slots – although the need to take a turn with these is clearly flagged up in contracts of employment.

The team has developed its own ways of dealing with this. But Nadia is alarmed, when she gets her first look at the figures, to see how much has been spent on agency staff by her predecessor. This is especially to cover weekends and bank holidays.

She wants to change this culture, and sets herself a target of reducing spend on agency staff by 10% in her first year. To achieve this, she needs the active cooperation of her team. How should she proceed?

Some options Nadia could consider:

- Consult informally to learn the 'history'.

- Call a team meeting with a one-item agenda.

- Produce figures to show the agency spend, as against total budgets.

- Indicate what other things could be done with this money, to improve things for residents and staff.

- Ask for suggestions for ways forward.

What happens next will depend on the way the meeting goes; the principles of even-handedness, consultation and the appropriate exercise of authority will need to determine Nadia's strategy.

Some other useful DIY planning tools

SWOT analysis – Strengths, Weaknesses, Opportunities and Threats

The SWOT analysis is one of the most useful simple planning tools you can employ. You can use a SWOT on your own, in pairs, in groups, in teams, or as a whole organisation. It is just about the best known and simplest DIY planning tool there is.

It can be used for team exercises or individual exercises on almost any theme. All that is required is a clear question, theme or objective.

Example

How to create and use a SWOT on: our performance last year.

All you need is a flip chart. Start with a clear focus: e.g. our publications list. You can either divide the page into quarters, or use a separate page for each heading, depending on size of topic. Then just let the ideas flow.

Take a piece of flip chart paper and draw a horizontal and a vertical line to make four quadrants. Title these as in the figure below.

Strengths	Weaknesses
Opportunities	Threats

Then take a quadrant at a time, and ask for contributions. No ideas are outlawed.

Stage 1: Strengths

Start with the positives: celebrate success!

Stage 2: Weaknesses

OK, so what did/do we do less well?

Look at these: what can we do to maximise our strengths and develop our skills for overcoming weak areas?

Stage 3: Opportunities

What could we be doing that we aren't doing now?

What new circumstances might create new openings for us?

Stage 4: Threats

What's in the wind? Competitors? Money worries? Loss of key team members? Problems with premises or equipment?

- Looking at the *strengths and weaknesses* of the list invites you to look *inward*
- Looking at the *opportunities and threats* invites you to look *outward*

There is a number of ways in which you can use the resulting ideas. Look at these lists, once you've generated them, and see what emerges for you. How can you use the synergy created by this exercise to 'think outside the box' on those opportunities? How can you handle the threats? Could you convert them into opportunities?

A STEP (or PEST) analysis

A companion to the SWOT is the STEP. This stands for:

- Social
- Technological
- Economic
- Political

This invites you to scan the wider environment in which your organisation operates. A STEP analysis invites you to look at your organisation from social, technological, economic, and political perspectives. How will these four factors impact on the work of your organisation in the year to come?

Sometimes you see this as a PESTL. The extra 'L' stands for 'legal'.

You can do this with regard to the Opportunities and Threats bit of your SWOT if that is helpful. Such an exercise prompts you to think about:

- New or changed circumstances since your last review
- Opportunities on which you could capitalise
- Ways to turn threats into opportunities

This invites you to create another matrix, this time looking out to the wider world.

Using the data

Both of these exercises need further work from you, to turn the data gleaned into usable material. Somehow you need to find ways to draw up priorities and action plans.

One energising way to do this in a team is to give people differently coloured sticky-notes, and invite them to stick them in colour-order on their favourite options for change. You can then see how the team choices are stacking up (see below).

From this sort of exercise a strong sense of team priorities is visibly built up, and 'ownership' of change is firmly established.

Brainstorming: free your mind

The use of this term has a long history, but it is now being challenged as possibly offensive. It may be best to think of the activity as mind-freeing. This means allowing everyone to contribute. The golden rule is to write everything down, without editing or censoring.

'Every new idea is born drowning.'

Some of the most popular products in the commercial sector have come about as a result of happy accidents. One well known example is the Post-it™ note. This was the result of a bright employee spotting a use for an adhesive that had apparently 'failed'.

The advantages of starting with a mind-freeing exercise will be that:

- You have involved everyone in the exercise of thinking about the task, product, team or organisation
- It can be energising and fun
- Creativity breeds creativity
- Everyone's opinions count
- You will have celebrated success together
- It can help build team spirit
- You will all have achieved new insights and perspectives which individuals could never have attained on their own
- Everyone is much more likely to 'buy in' to the resulting plan

Prioritising

Of course you can't just leave it there. What actions are you going take? And in what order? You will need to prioritise.

Say you are looking at the opportunities for your team in the year ahead. You need to come to a shared agreement about which to pursue. One thing that works well is to:

- Divide the opportunities into clusters
- Put each cluster on one page of a flip chart
- Stick the flip chart pages round the office wall
- Give each team member three sticky-notes marked 1, 2, 3 (you can give them different colours if you want to get classy; say red for top priority, green second, blue third)
- Ask them to go round the room, sticking their sticky-notes beside their preferred priorities

You will get a good visual picture of where the votes are going. You may find everyone gives more thought to their choices. They will also be in a good position to see if others share their views, or if they are lone voices. Of course you will need to give some thought in advance to what is manageable and what is not: apparently open and democratic consultation exercises that are then ignored by managers breed cynicism faster than most things.

The value of away days

The value of getting away as a team to plan and review can scarcely be overemphasised. If you sense that there is a big policy issue coming up, or something about the way the team is working that is unresolved, or getting in the way of good practice or good relations, then consider an away day. It does not have to be a whole day. It does not have to cost much – or anything, if you can find a free venue – except the cost of providing cover for your usual work. But the value of taking time to consider and plan together, away from the press of immediate business, can be immense.

Case study

An IT team wants to use its away day to look at refreshing the way it works. Things have changed: new equipment, new demands. There is a growing demand for their services, but no money to employ additional staff. Existing staff are feeling weary, jaded and underbriefed.

The team leader, Omar, wants to use the day to consider how they can make best use of their limited resources, whilst giving the team a good time, and renewing commitment and motivation. How would you advise Omar to plan the day?

Some options Omar might consider:

- Book time and space away from the office, in good time.

- Make sure everyone can attend: this means booking the date well ahead, and keeping it sacrosanct. Don't forget part time staff: they can feel marginalised if a date is selected that they can't manage.

- If funds are short, consider a space which won't require payment, but which offers some kind of 'treat' aspect. Perhaps out of doors if it is summer time? Try at all costs to pay for lunch.

- Put up a suggestions sheet in a prominent place for staff to contribute ideas and topics for the agenda, with a deadline well ahead of the event to aid planning.

- Consider a 'guest speaker' if the team seeks input on any new developments. Select good communicators, and brief them so that they don't speak too long. Encourage them to offer a stimulating pump-primer and then to take questions.

- Avoid lengthy PowerPoint presentations. Encourage interaction, by every means possible. Enable all to contribute, and ensure all feel heard.

- Divide the time up, so that at least half (perhaps more) is spent on 'thinking outside the box'. Provide opportunities to be creative, and bring along a flip chart, and plenty of coloured pens and coloured sticky-notes.

- Avoid 'cheesy games' unless absolutely sure they will go down well, and have a point which is clear to all.

- Ensure that the day comes to a satisfactory conclusion, with a sense of achievement. Ensure that the 'next steps' are clear, with commonly agreed and realistic deadlines, and that they will be actioned.

- Celebrate the effort! If at all possible, finish with a treat.

Project planning

There is no particular magic about project planning. But it's helpful to think systematically, right at the outset, about what's involved.

Project checklist:

- Overall aim: can you express this in one sentence? Start with a 'to...'
- Desired outcomes: what are they?
- Resources: people
- Resources: budget
- Resources: technology, equipment, space
- Timescale
- Deadlines
- Success factors: how will you know when you have succeeded?
- Monitoring: methods and timeframes
- Evaluation: who? and how?

Timelines

Working out what needs to be done when, and in what order, to bring the project in within its deadline, is a crucial skill. Some people use computer software to do this. If you are working on your own, a simple timeline, working backwards from your deadline, may be all you need. But if you are working with others, one or two other tips may be useful.

Say you have to organise a conference in a year's time. You know you will have to get the leaflet out by Christmas to have your bookings in by March, say. So what do you need to do before you can get your leaflet out?

You may have to:

- Decide the aims of the conference
- Decide the theme or topic, and find a title
- Decide the budget
- Decide the numbers – delegates and speakers and others

- Decide the date/duration
- Search for a venue with the right facilities
- Visit a few venues
- Book a venue
- Design your programme
- Book your speakers, workshop leaders etc.
- Design your leaflet
- Research mailshot options
- Decide the print run
- Get your leaflet to the printers

Task-boarding

Getting the tasks clear is one thing, putting them in order is another. You will find that some tasks must be done before others. If you are doing this in a team, it can help to:

- Write each task on a separate sticky-note
- Stick the notes on a white board or similar, in the order in which they must be done: you will find some clump together, while others are 'one-off' jobs
- If you allow yourself a day or two for this, you are bound to come up with other tasks, which you can then slot in

Now you should have your tasks arranged in a sensible order.

Gantt charts

A Gantt chart (called after its inventor, Henry Gantt) is simply a way of schematising this, in a spreadsheet format. There may be 'project' programs on your computer that will do this for you, or you can make your own, using Excel for instance. Here's how you do it:

- You list all the tasks down the left hand column of the chart, with the months (or weeks) along the top
- Because you have worked out which tasks depend on which others for their completion, you can plot the order in which they should come

- Once you've done this, it's best to work backwards
- Show how long each task is likely to take (allow plenty of slippage time!)
- Then you have a graphic representation of key milestone dates, and of what should be going on, at any time, if the project is to be brought in on time
- Very useful if you are working on anything which involves more than one person – or even just for yourself, if you're handling anything long or complex
- Try it for a project you know well. It's easier, and more helpful than it sounds!

You can use Gantt charts both for routine tasks which happen time after time, and for one-off projects.

The example below shows the chart compiled by a training organisation to show the steps towards getting a training leaflet mailed out.

Tip: KISS (keep it simple, sweetheart!)

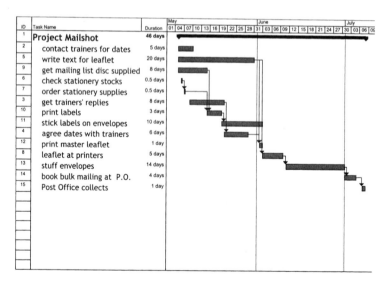

A sample Gantt chart

4
Motivating and managing individuals

'Employees leave managers, not companies.' (Graeme Buckingham)

Why do people stay in their jobs?

Research shows that people stay when they:

- Have a manager who demonstrates interest and care
- Have effective and appropriate feedback
- Know what is expected of them
- Have a role that fits their ability

Let's take these in order.

A manager who demonstrates interest and care

This isn't about endlessly asking people how they are feeling. It's about:

- Ensuring that regular one-to-one sessions take place
- Taking an interest in staff as people, not just as employees
- Taking an active interest in the individual's professional development
- Listening with empathy
- Always keeping confidences
- Being supportive and encouraging

It's also about recognising that, in the words of the song:

'It ain't what you do it's the way that you do it.

It ain't what you say it's the way that you say it.'

More of this below!

Offering effective and appropriate feedback

Most of us want to know how we are doing, so that we can grow and develop in our roles. Yet many of us fear giving feedback.

Feedback can be positive as well as negative. Think about this for a moment.

- Most of us do 80% of our jobs well, most of the time
- This means there is some room for improvement on about 20%
- But 80% of the feedback we receive at work is usually about that 20%
- When were you last praised for a good piece of work?
- Does your office foster a blame culture?
- Is it surprising we fear both offering and receiving feedback?

So the good manager will:

- Notice and praise good work, as often as possible
- Always pass on positive feedback, as soon as possible
- Praise in public, criticise in private
- Praise sincerely and concretely: e.g. 'that was an excellent presentation: the overheads were particularly useful, and the trustees were very impressed.' Not just 'You're wonderful.'
- Start with the positive
- Ask questions first, to clarify understanding
- Offer negative feedback with respect
- Work from first hand evidence, not hearsay
- Own the feedback
- Use first person statements like: 'I have noticed that…'
- Focus on the behaviour, not the person
- Engage the staff member in considering options for change
- Work towards win–win solutions

'Catch people doing something right.'

Timing is particularly important: where possible, offer feedback as soon as possible after the relevant event. Take every opportunity you can to offer positive feedback. Make sure that it is both sincere and specific.

If you need to give negative feedback, consider whether you need to do it immediately, or not. If immediately (where, for example, confidentiality is being threatened, or clients' safety is being compromised) then find a private spot if you can – as long as this does not mean you are regularly taking people aside for 'a quick word'.

Consider holding less important feedback for the supervision session. Never store up criticism for the annual appraisal, however. Remember:

Criticism + storage = resentment

Resentment + appraisal = trouble!

Most of us want to do our best at work. Staff who feel respected and valued will welcome feedback which enables them to do their jobs to the best of their ability.

Giving criticism

- It's OK for you to want people to improve their performance
- Approach it in a problem solving way rather than blaming
- Don't try to make the person seem small or inadequate

Case study

Magda's time keeping has become very erratic. She used to be punctual and reliable, but recently you have noticed that she has been coming in late, leaving early, and taking long lunch hours. She has not given any explanation of these changes, so you don't know whether she is having any personal difficulties: certainly she has not mentioned any particular domestic problems in your hearing.

As far as you know, there are no problems with her work, and she is getting everything done. However, you feel this is something you need to tackle – if only because a number of team members have noticed, and started to show some resentment.

How will you plan to raise this at your up-coming supervision session?

Some options you could consider:

- Consider carefully whether you need to raise this at all.

- Ensure you have your evidence ready, before the meeting. This may feel like snooping, but it's important not to raise this concern unless you have specific instances in view. Vague impressions are not enough, nor is hearsay.

- Start with the positives about Magda's work.

- Ask Magda how things have been going – leave this open-ended.

- Continue with gentle open questions, to explore how she sees things.

- If she does not mention any problems, start with 'I have noticed that…' And bring in your evidence. Ask questions to check out your understanding. Ask: 'Were you aware of that?'

- Use 'I' language, and 'we' language. Avoid 'You always…'

- Consider carefully whether or not to mention third parties. It may be better not to.

- Stress any pre-existing policy on time keeping. (Does your organisation offer flexible working? Could you consider it as a team option?)

- If she does share personal information, stress confidentiality, offer to check out policy if appropriate (don't promise compassionate leave, for example, only to find your organisation doesn't offer it in these circumstances), and offer support. Start to problem-solve together.

- Recognise the limits of your responsibility, and your right to know. You are responsible for supporting and managing performance at work, not for sorting out personal problems.

- Agree an action plan, and a review date.

- Finish on a positive note.

- Use open gestures and an even tone
- Keep it factual – say what you know
- Ask for a response 'Were you aware of that?'
- Ask for a solution – 'What ideas do you have?'
- Summarise and list action points

Knowing what is expected: staff appraisal systems

Does your organisation run a staff appraisal scheme? Increasingly, organisations are devising performance management schemes that involve regular supervision sessions, for one-to-one feedback and discussion between staff and their managers, underpinned by an appraisal system.

Appraisal schemes usually offer a more formal (often annual) opportunity to:

- Share feedback about how staff feel about their jobs
- Assess performance against agreed objectives for the past year
- Celebrate success and look at things which did not go so well
- Agree objectives, with any associated targets, for the year ahead
- Look at training and other staff development needs
- Review the job description, and agree any changes

There are a number of different models in use:

- Some systems are formally linked to pay
- Some systems involve the formal seeking of feedback about the staff member's performance from others (e.g. colleagues and peers, subordinates, senior managers, peer organisations, other stakeholders). This is often called 360 degree appraisal

Appraisal schemes usually involve some paperwork. There should be an appraisal policy, guidelines (and training) for appraisers, and forms to structure the interview process. Ideally there will be a form for the appraisee to complete, prior to the interview, which will encourage them to reflect on what has gone well over the year, and on what has gone less well. These work best if they are fairly loosely structured, with open 'prompt' questions. Avoid box-ticking, if you have any choice in the matter.

No surprises

Of course, managers are appraising their team members informally all the time. It is vital that feedback is offered as near in time to the occasion that prompted it as possible. Appraisals should contain no surprises. That is why regular one-to-one supervision sessions are so vital. These are the 'pit stops' between the big, more formal, annual appraisal sessions.

Having a role that fits your ability

Recruitment

How were you recruited to your job? What did you think of the process? Some organisations have got recruitment down to a fine art; for others, there may be room for improvement.

Staffing costs count for far the greatest outlay in most organisations. Recruitment itself is expensive, in terms of time and reputation as well as money. It pays to do all you can to get it right, to get the best appointees you can, and to make the process successful so that you aren't faced with having to do it all over again sooner than you'd planned.

If all goes to plan:

- The **job description** will be clear enough for you to know what you are putting in for when you apply
- The **person specification** will be clear enough so that you know what skills and experience levels they are looking for, you won't waste your, or their, time, and you won't end up feeling over or underqualified for the role
- The **terms and conditions of employment** will be clearly spelled out, so there are no surprises

- The **interview process** will give you both the chance to make sure you know enough – you about them, or them about you – to know whether it will work out well
- The **selection process** will be fair and will provide equal opportunities for all to shine
- And, for the successful candidate, the **induction process** will be thought through, thorough, supportive and relevant

That way, there's the best chance of a successful appointment, and a happy and motivated staff member.

Managing underperformance

But things don't always run smoothly. What can you do when you have to manage someone whose skills and abilities have been outstripped by the pace of change in their area of work? Sometimes you may inherit staff members whose roles have outgrown them. Performance is suffering, and you have to act. A good example might be the double entry bookkeeper whose computer skills are not up to the challenge of the new computerised accountancy package. What are your options in this sort of situation?

- **Training.** This is the obvious first step. Sometimes this is all that is needed, and where your staff member is keen to reskill, it's the obvious answer. It's not always going to work, however, or perhaps your colleague is resistant to change? Perhaps they've been with the organisation a long time, have served it well and loyally, and you don't want to force the issue
- **Flexibility in job design**. If you can, it may work best to find ways to redistribute the work. This may be inconvenient or expensive: it's a judgement call. But it may avoid an even more difficult situation. Try to be as flexible as you can
- **Capability policy**. Some organisations have developed policies to deal with these and similar situations, where staff are not performing well, but this is not a disciplinary matter. The ultimate sanction for the disciplinary policy is termination of employment. The ultimate step in capability policy too may be termination of employment, but the grounds will be different. It will be incapacity, rather than

unwillingness or indiscipline, which sets the process in motion. Similarly to the disciplinary process, it will be vital to have a policy in place, and to have observed it scrupulously, should such a case come to an employment tribunal. Seek HR help: you can't do this on your own!

Motivating individuals and teams

'You can never change another person. You can only inspire people to want to change themselves.'

Much of the success of your work as a manager will depend on the quality of the people in your team. You may feel that much of this is outside your control. You can't recruit everyone anew: you will inherit some people. But you will influence the morale and productivity of your team significantly by the way you set about understanding their strengths and weaknesses, understanding their circumstances, learning what rewards they seek at work, developing their skills and competencies, improving people's jobs, and supervising and appraising them.

How well do you know your colleagues?

What rewards do the individuals you work with seek at work? What drives them?

Think of three key individuals for whose work you are responsible. Which of these factors do you think might motivate them? Choose five:

- Good wages or salary
- The prospect of promotion
- Getting as much free time as possible
- Flexible working hours
- Family friendly policies
- Working with the team: having fun
- The satisfaction of turning out high quality work
- Contributing to a worthwhile enterprise
- Working for this particular organisation
- Working for this particular person
- The opportunity to travel

- Regular, predictable work-flow
- Exciting, challenging work
- Learning new skills at work
- Being creative
- Following procedures
- Gaining personal status or power
- Having some freedom to decide how they work
- Being told exactly what to do
- Being respected by colleagues
- Being respected by others
- Getting on well with customers/clients
- Good working conditions
- The location of our workplace

If you are honest, you probably found this hard. It's hard to pick five, just for yourself: harder still for your colleagues. And you will have been aware that you were second-guessing much of the time.

If you don't know, make a point of asking. We can often make the mistake of thinking everyone is just like us. Often you can easily make small changes in working conditions for people that will make a big difference to how they feel about coming to work, without reneging on your responsibilities or showing favouritism.

Case study

David has just been promoted to the post of finance manager. He now manages Lucy, the finance assistant. Lucy is in her mid thirties, some seven years older than David. He thinks she has children, but he isn't sure.

David has been concerned about the number of days of sick leave Lucy takes. Her work is good, she gets on well with colleagues, and she seems conscientious but she is regularly away – for as much as a couple of days a month.

David does not know Lucy very well. He knows nothing about the rest of her life. He feels he must tackle the sick leave issue, but is dreading bringing it up. He worries that Lucy may feel embarrassed talking to him about her health – even though he doubts whether she is 'really' ill. How might David tackle this?

Some options David might consider:

- Seek help! David needs to find out whether his organisation has a sickness management policy, and if so, what it says. Many organisations are developing such policies, which can take some of the awkwardness out of handling individual cases. Often a return to work interview is involved.

- Does his organisation have a human resources (personnel) department? If so, consult. Are there links with occupational health services, for instance?

- Talk the situation through with his own manager. Can she or he help?

- The cause of the regular absences needs to be established. The best way is the straightforward one. David needs to collect the evidence of Lucy's absence record, and present her with it, gently asking whether there is any long-term problem he should know about. Alternatively, David may wish to hand the problem over to a senior woman manager, if he feels uncomfortable talking to Lucy about her medical history.

- If Lucy appears embarrassed to discuss things, it may be worth asking whether she would find it easier to talk to a woman manager anyway. Perhaps she has a menstrual problem. Is there a senior woman manager with whom David could discuss how to handle things, and who may be prepared to intervene?

- It may be that Lucy has a different health problem entirely, but one she has not yet liked to mention. It could even be a work-related issue: something connected with the equipment or office environment perhaps. Could Lucy's difficulty be stress-related? David needs to check this out, and ensure that there is not an underlying health and safety issue. Again, specialist help is probably needed.

- Could it be that there is an underlying capability issue? Or is Lucy unhappy at work in some other way? Is she being bullied, perhaps?

- It sounds as though David needs to get to know Lucy as an individual a little better in any case. Maybe her absences have other causes entirely. Are there domestic issues that it might be helpful to know about? Although absence for reasons other than illness, and without prior agreement, is often a disciplinary matter, it may be that Lucy finds herself in an impossible situation of some sort. If so, could David support Lucy in thinking things through, and in working out strategies for managing some of the conflicts between home and work responsibilities?

- David does need to tackle this, but he doesn't have to do it alone.

Motivators and hygiene factors

Frederick Herzberg wrote a classic study on motivation in which he distinguished between what he called motivators and hygiene factors.

The motivators were things like:

- Achievement
- Recognition
- The work itself
- Responsibility
- Advancement/promotion
- Growth

These are the factors that produce job satisfaction.

He distinguished them from the so-called hygiene factors, which included things like:

- Company policy and administration
- Relationship with supervisor
- Working conditions
- Salary
- Relationships with peers and subordinates
- Status and security

These factors alone could not motivate. But if they weren't right, they could produce job dissatisfaction.

It's interesting to note, especially thinking about salaries and the current debate around performance related pay, that more money alone will not motivate. Nor will potted palms in the company HQ. But if you feel you are hard done by in terms of your peers in other organisations, or your working conditions are truly awful, your job satisfaction is likely to suffer, no matter how passionate you are about the work. Managers need to take note!

The art of delegation

Delegation is frequently done badly. People often see it as dumping. Tasks thrown at you with no briefing; tasks thrown at you without your agreement; tasks thrown at you that exceed your capability, skills or powers; tasks thrown at you with impossibly tight deadlines, or no guideline as to deadline or priority; your boss being unclear about what it is they actually want achieved; vagueness about money or resources; changing goal posts; vagueness about levels of delegated authority: the list of possible pitfalls is a long one.

But, as a manager, you certainly need to be able to delegate. You would not need a team if you could do everything yourself. Amongst other things, a delegated project can 'grow' a staff member, and provide a great opportunity for them to make a big success of it, have something new to put on the CV, *and* get a job done for you. WIN–WIN.

Many new managers find delegating hard: do any of these sound like you?

- 'It takes too long. It's quicker to do it myself.'
- 'My team don't have the experience to do a good enough job.'
- 'She won't/can't do it like I did.'
- 'He'll make too many mistakes.'
- 'It won't be quite right.'
- 'I don't want to lose track of things.'

Learning to trust colleagues, and to 'let go', can be hard. Settling for a 'good enough' job is difficult, if you're conscious of being a bit of a perfectionist. But sometimes it's the right thing to do.

The five anchors of delegation

1. **Describe the outcome.** Make sure the person is clear about what you want them to achieve in the delegated task both in terms of the process as well as the outcome. If you have a lot of confidence in them, you may feel able to leave the process to them and simply describe the outcome, but if in doubt – explain.

   For each task delegated specify:

   - the desired outcome

- any timescales involved – both end times and critical path times
- the resources available
- any other colleagues who must/might be consulted/involved
- the processes and procedures to be followed

2. **Provide the necessary tools.** Make sure they have everything they need in order to do the task as well as possible. This may mean freeing up their time or helping them to reprioritise. It may mean training or who to go to for advice. It may mean simply ensuring that they have access to the only computer in the office when they need it!

3. **Set up check points.** If the delegated task is new to your staff member, it is a good idea to ask them to come back and check with you before committing themselves or the organisation to any major decisions. How often you ask them to do this and in what level of detail will depend on how much confidence you have in them in the first place.

4. **Follow up and coach.** A delegated task means a learning opportunity for the staff member – otherwise it feels like dumping! Make sure that you support the learning process by reinforcing good work through praise and encouragement and working on weaknesses by positive suggestions and discussion.

5. **Praise in public.** If you have delegated something that went well, make sure you give credit to the person who did the work. If you have delegated something that went badly, make sure you take the blame yourself. This is part of what being 'tough at the top' means.

Different levels of delegation

It's also most important to specify how much authority and responsibility you are giving to the staff member.

1. **Carry out the work under my constant supervision.** Most commonly used with new members of staff. The delegator is in constant contact with the task until the staff member is able to perform it reliably themselves.

2. **Carry out the work in this way and consult with me before taking any action.** Both the process and the outcomes are specified by the delegator. The staff member will plan the work but must consult before committing themselves or the organisation to any risky decisions.

3. **Carry out the work as you see fit but report back to me before taking any action.** Here the process is left to the staff member's discretion but the delegator retains final control before the big decisions are taken.

4. **Carry out the work and report back regularly on what you've done.** Here, the process is left to the staff member's discretion and they have freedom to act but must report after the fact. This level will tend to be used only with people in whom you have a reasonable level of confidence.

5. **Carry out the work and report back only when you encounter difficulties.** This is the level of delegation we have with our senior teams. It is assumed that their decision making and performance levels are problem free unless they tell us otherwise.

6. **This is your project – achieve the objective(s) in whatever way you see fit.** This is the highest level of delegation and, in reality, used very rarely. At this level the staff member has complete discretion and carries complete responsibility (though not accountability) for the task.

As a rule of thumb, the further down this series of levels you get the better, as long as you remain confident that the staff member's efforts will be crowned with success. Most of us would prefer to be given our heads with a project, and dislike feeling that the boss is breathing down our necks. At the same time, it's not fair to leave an inexperienced staff member to sink or swim, nor is it fair to wash your hands of a failed project delegated by you. You remain accountable. If the project is a great success, this must be put down to their credit. If not, then you need to take responsibility. It's tough at the top!

Case study

Marsha is services manager in a local housing management office. Her director asked her to undertake a piece of research some three months ago, but somehow she has never found the time to make a start. At the time, there was no deadline.

Marsha has just had a meeting with the director who has asked her how the work is going, and whether the final report will be ready to take to the board meeting in two months' time. She has not liked to tell her director that she has not started yet. She is going on two weeks' annual leave, starting tomorrow.

Marsha has an excellent new assistant manager called Paul. She comes straight out of the meeting and hands Paul the project file. So far, there is nothing in it, except the director's original email. She tells Paul to make it his top priority.

How is Paul likely to feel about this? What should Marsha do to help?

Some options Marsha could consider:

- If she values Paul, she should rethink at once! Paul is likely to feel put upon and resentful, however capable he is. However, given the right preparation, this could be a great opportunity for Paul to demonstrate his capabilities. She could sell it as such.

- Marsha needs to find a way of letting the director know she has not started the work. She should explain that she has delegated the groundwork to Paul in her holiday absence, and seek the director's help in supporting Paul whilst she is away.

- She needs to make time to talk through the project with Paul right away, starting with the aims and objectives, and ensuring he understands as much of the big picture as possible. She needs to discuss with him what he can reasonably achieve in her absence, and let him know to whom he can turn whilst she is away. On her return, she should let everyone know what a great job Paul has done, and encourage him to see the project through if possible. She needs to recognise his loyalty, value his work, and thank him personally.

5
Leading your team

How is your team's motivation?

Here are some symptoms that might indicate poor motivation. Do any of these apply in your team?

	✓
Low productivity	❑
Absenteeism	❑
Poor time-keeping	❑
High staff turnover	❑
Poor quality work	❑
Customer/client complaints	❑
Low team morale	❑
Interpersonal conflicts within the team	❑
Conflicts with management	❑
Inflexible attitudes to change	❑
Bad relations with other parts of the organisation	❑

If one or two individuals get disgruntled, they can often undermine the spirit of the whole team. Can you think of times when you have been in teams like this? What solutions worked, or might have worked, to restore the team spirit?

Things you might do:

- Be more visible. Are you away too much?
- Ensure you make time for one-to-one sessions
- Ensure you make time for (and attend!) staff meetings
- Develop your listening skills

- Communicate! Make sure people have the information they need

- Consult, consult, consult. Make it clear that colleagues' views matter

- Celebrate success and achievement: encourage a celebratory culture

- Tackle problems and difficulties as soon as you are aware of them. Don't leave things to fester

- Stay focused yet flexible

- Be prepared to mediate between fractious colleagues

- Walk the talk. Be a good role model

'If you want to inspire your team, first inspire yourself.'

Team processes

All teams go through certain processes during their lifecycles. It's worth knowing that these are the likely stages in the life of any group of people brought together to focus on a specific task:

- **Forming.** The group comes together. Individuals may feel anxious, stressed, enthusiastic, switched off, or any number of other things.

- **Norming.** The individuals in the group check each other out. Who are the 'natural' leaders? What strengths are there in the group? Where are the weak links? Will I enjoy being part of this group? Will I feel left out? What will I be able to contribute? What do I need, to feel included?

- **Storming.** There may be some trials of strength, bids for attention, staking out territory and roles, leadership bids, challenges, conflicts, some jockeying for position. Some members may be very vocal, others passive and silent.

- **Performing.** Only when the group has got through these phases will its members be ready to give of their best and achieve the task. In some groups, for instance where members already know each other fairly well, the early phases may be over quickly. In others, there may be a sense that the group is 'stuck' at an earlier stage and can't start performing.

- **Mourning.** When the task is complete and the group has to disband there will be some sadness. Rituals help to mark closure: like rites of passage. The wise team leader will recognise this and celebrate. Mark the completion of the task with some sort of party or event. Similarly, if a team member leaves, and/or a new one joins there will be some loss to recognise. Don't be surprised if the team falters at this point. Be ready to support, listen and encourage.

Running effective team meetings: some suggestions

- **Meet regularly** as a team. It cannot be a team if people are isolated, and only make contact by phone, email, or one-off chats
- **Chairing**: the chair should:
  - Encourage both task and process (see below)
  - See that there is a proper agenda or logical flow
  - Allow time for each issue
  - Ensure everyone is heard
  - Keep the meeting to time
  - Ensure there is a record of action points, circulated quickly
- Team meetings need proper **agendas.** You might consider creating one which states:
  - Topic: what's the issue?
  - Initiator: the person wanting it discussed
  - Purpose: what it's broadly about
  - Timescale: the amount of time it will require
  - Outcome: is it for decision, discussion or information?

Effective meetings checklist

How successful are your team meetings? You could try rating yourself from 1–5 on this checklist, where 1 = 'We're great at this' and 5 = 'This definitely needs attention':

✓ We know what we are there for

✓ The agenda items are relevant and all the important items are on the agenda

✓ There is fresh discussion on each item

✓ Everyone is able to participate and contribute

✓ We reach consensus on most items

✓ When we disagree, this is explicit and the reasons are clear

✓ The meetings take about the right length of time

✓ At the end of the meeting, we've all learned something and we know more about what we've got to do next

✓ The notes of the meeting reflect what we thought happened and are circulated quickly

Task, team and individual

John Adair, a well-known management theorist, wrote about what he called action-centred leadership. A good leader must consider three different things, all at the same time:

- **Task**: the job in hand
- **Team**: the group that comes together to achieve the task
- **Individual**: the team member

Lose sight of any of these three at your peril! If you are exclusively task focused, both the team and individual team members will suffer and lose motivation. If you are exclusively individual focused, the job won't get done, and team members will get frustrated. If you are exclusively team focused, individuals may feel ignored, and targets will be missed.

It is helpful to separate task-focused behaviours from the kinds of behaviours that encourage people to give of their best.

The **task** is anything which the group comes together to achieve.

Maintenance involves the building up and nurturing of the relationships between group members, and is vital to the achievement of the task.

Case study

Errol is a new team leader. His team has never previously had meetings, and most staff say they do not want them. They just want to be left alone to get on with their work. Jeff says he used to work in an office where the Monday morning team meetings used to be a 'complete waste of time'. Ron says there will never be a good time to get everybody together; he's out such a lot, visiting projects around the country. Lee and Kim are not keen, but agree it would be good to discuss things 'now and then'.

Sheila, however, is keen to meet regularly. 'We are all becoming over-reliant on email. I never speak to anyone any more, it seems. It would be good to get together to agree new procedures, get regular briefings from you about the big picture, and review how things are going. It doesn't have to be every week!'

Errol thinks it would be a good idea too. How would you advise him to take things forward?

Some options Errol could consider:

- Find a time for the team to go out to lunch together, perhaps. Or at least find some time away from the day-to-day business to consider how communication is working in the team, and whether regular meetings would have any merit.

- Recognise the strength of everyone's different positions. 'I quite take Jeff's point... And Sheila's too. And Ron is learning so much out in the field that we never get a chance to share. How can we take things forward?'

- It might be an opportunity for a quick SWOT exercise, just on 'our communication'. Errol needs to recognise that there's a risk that the group may feel the usefulness of meetings is NOT proven, though...

- If meetings are going to work, it's important that everyone feels there's something in it for them. Errol must guard against imposing, and seek to negotiate 'buy-in' for the idea.

- It would be important to agree how the agenda would be drawn up, how chairing would be organised, timings and time limits, and record keeping. Good will can drain away into the sand if these things are not thought through.

- Errol may want to propose, say, a monthly meeting structure, at a regular time everyone could make, for a six-month trial period. It would need to be diarised there and then. At the end of that time, the team could review whether or not the meetings had worked for them.

If the **task** is concentrated upon at the expense of nurturing relationships in the group, then the cooperation necessary for completing the task does not develop, and the task will not be completed satisfactorily.

If the **maintenance** of relationships is concentrated upon at the expense of the task, the achievement of the task suffers setbacks, people lose motivation and have a sense of frustration. Task and maintenance need to go hand in hand.

Task orientated behaviour

- Proposing: initiating ideas, suggestions, courses of action relevant to the task
- Seeking information: asking for facts, opinions or clarification from other members of the group
- Giving information: offering facts, opinions or clarification concerning the task
- Summarising/building: restating succinctly the content of the previous discussion, and extending a proposal made by someone else

Maintenance orientated behaviour

- Encouraging: being warm, friendly or supportive of others by verbal and/or non-verbal means
- Gatekeeping: opening gates – positively attempting to involve others in the discussion; closing gates – excluding, cutting off or interrupting others, where it becomes necessary to forward the business
- Harmonising: being prepared to compromise and actively accommodate others in order to preserve group harmony

Task orientated behaviours are 'getting the job done' behaviours.

Maintenance orientated behaviours are 'looking after people' behaviours.

Good team leaders practise both.

(Adapted from *Once Upon a Group Exercises*, 4M publications)

Case study

Rosie has a major conference to organise in two weeks' time. She is getting stressed, and so are her two team members, Ian and Shelley. They are working every evening until 7 or 8 p.m., and they will have to do so again over the conference itself. The conference takes place over a weekend (Friday to Sunday).

Ian has come to Rosie to ask for some time off in lieu. Rosie has not come across this term before, and doesn't know how to handle the request. Her own manager is on annual leave. She snaps at Ian that she'll do her best, but she can't promise anything...

What suggestions would you make to Rosie, to support her team?

Some options for Rosie to consider:

- Time off in lieu (or TOIL) is certainly a familiar concept in most organisations where overtime is not payable. It is a way of making reparation to people who have worked long hours, above their contractual obligations, particularly if this involves evening and weekend working. Every organisation needs to have given some thought to how it will handle TOIL requests, and indeed to offering TOIL in advance, in circumstances like this.

- Rosie needs to find someone other than her manager with whom to check whether the organisation has a policy, and if so what it is.

- If there is no policy, it would certainly be reasonable for Rosie to make an agreement with Ian and Shelley, to show the extent to which she values their good will. She may think it appropriate to apologise for snapping, and not having thought of this herself!

- Rosie may want to consult both of them as to what they think would be reasonable, in the short term, and to go along with this if she agrees, or to negotiate a compromise if she does not. It's certainly worth settling this now. Then when her manager returns she can explain what she has done and why, and they can discuss a way forward for the organisation as a whole.

6
You and your management style

There are many grids and matrices charting the different management styles. This is just one. It comes with a health warning. You should not regard it as an attempt to label people, or put them in pigeon-holes. We are all capable of a repertoire of different behaviours, and few of us demonstrate just one of these styles, all the time. It's helpful, though, to become self aware, to recognise your own 'default' style, so that you can know when and if it would be appropriate to make a change.

" IS THIS A GOOD TIME TO ASK FOR A RISE ? "

Six management styles

1. **Coercive**: seeks immediate compliance: tight control, clear direction, uses negative feedback, no negotiation.

When?

- in a crisis
- when protocol must be followed to the letter
- when all else has failed

Least effective:

- as a long term strategy with capable, motivated employees

2. Authoritative: articulates a clear vision and direction, seeks employee perspective whilst retaining control, uses positive and negative feedback to enhance employee motivation, sets clear standards and goals and monitors these.

When?

- when communicating and explaining vision
- when the manager is the 'expert'
- with new employees

Least effective:

- if used extensively with an experienced team
- when trying to promote self management and participative decision making

3. Affiliative: focuses on promoting harmony amongst team before achievement of task, takes steps to meet the needs of the 'whole' person, identifies opportunities for positive feedback and avoids challenging performance related problems.

When?

- when tasks are routine and performance is satisfactory
- with diverse and conflicting groups
- with employees needing personal support

Least effective:

- with employees who are task orientated
- when negative performance feedback is needed to raise standards/achieve targets

4. Democratic: builds commitment and consensus, gives teams a full role in setting direction, planning and goals, emphasises consensus, consults regularly, listens attentively, rewards team rather than 'stars'.

When?

- when time is on your side
- in team building
- to build commitment and 'ownership'
- with experienced employees who share common concerns

Least effective:

- if there is a risk staff will decide something you can't accept
- if the situation requires that you take a lead

5. Pacesetting: leads by example. Works individually, rather than as a team leader, to a very high standard. Delegates demanding tasks only to outstanding performers, and controls poor performers tightly. Promotes individualised effort rather than teamwork.

When?

- with self starters who are themselves pacemakers
- with poor performers who are on their way out
- when it is necessary to work side by side with the team

Least effective:

- when employees want feedback or help to improve performance
- when staff want access to their manager
- when direction for the team is not clearly established

6. Coaching: aims for long term professional development of staff. Helps identify strengths and weaknesses in performance. Uses listening and open-ended questions to help employees to problem-solve. See mistakes as learning opportunities.

When?

- with staff interested in career development

- to encourage staff to find their own solutions
- to support risk-taking and innovation

Least effective:

- with new staff who lack experience
- when explicit direction is needed
- in a crisis

(Adapted from a model used by Hay McBer Consulting)

As this shows, there is no one 'right' style. It all depends on circumstances. The **coercive** style, for instance, may sound unappealing, but when there is a crisis, it may be the only appropriate style to use.

The **democratic** style sounds like a good thing, but don't use it where there is a danger people may come up with a decision you can't take forward. That way, they'll feel cheated and devalued.

The **affiliative** style might sound warm and appealing, but be careful when you have to deal with disciplinary problems.

It's helpful to try to identify your own default style. You may be able to see, then, where you may need to make changes. These may be permanent, or just gear changes for particular circumstances, to deal with situations at work you are finding particularly challenging. It's always useful to be able to operate comfortably in more than one register.

Conflict resolution

Conflicts are part of organisational life. Indeed they are a healthy part. Conflict often forces people to think through their positions, in ways they have not had to do before. If teams always agree, they can get stale; group-think takes over, and there is nothing to challenge them to think through their practice, and perhaps come up with better ways of doing things.

Yet conflicts which are not well handled, which are avoided, or left to fester till the parties become entrenched, can do damage to teams. Your strategies for handling conflict will make a big difference to your success as a manager, and to the success of your team.

So how do you deal with differences of view in the team?

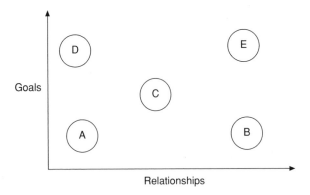

What's your default style?

In the figure above, the vertical axis denotes the extent to which you are task and goal driven. The horizontal axis denotes the extent to which you are relationship driven. Both of these things matter. The most helpful position for managers is to demonstrate high scores for **both** task achievement **and** relationship maintenance.

Next time you have a difficult issue to resolve in the team, ask yourself where you are likely to stand. Which of these positions are you likeliest to adopt?

A = **Avoiding.** If you adopt the ostrich position wherever possible, and would do anything rather than have a fight, you are likely to be an avoider. This is, in a way, the worst position to be in. You do not mind either way, and tend to keep your head in the sand.

B = **Accommodating.** You set a high store by good working relationships, and that is a good and important thing. However, could it be that you sometimes back off from difficult situations, rather than offend? Or that you duck or fudge unpopular but necessary decisions, to keep colleagues sweet? You may need to accept the need to exert your authority sometimes.

C = **Compromising.** This sounds like a woolly position to find yourself in, but sometimes it can be the right position for all that. You are motivated by *both* goal achievement *and* the maintenance of harmonious relations, but by neither to excess.

When things get tough, and there's no harm done by giving ground, the wise manager will do so.

D = **Competing.** Is winning important for you? Are you, if you are honest, a bit of a slave-driver? Do you need to get your own way at all costs? Be careful! If management is the art of getting extraordinary results from ordinary people, you may need to reflect on what matters to colleagues, as well as to yourself. It's no good exceeding your targets by 50% if all your team leave in the process.

E = **Collaborating.** This is the best position to adopt, wherever you can. You are setting high values on *both* goal-achievement *and* relationships. Co-Laborate means 'work with'. It's a win–win position. Congratulations if this is where you usually find yourself.

If you find you have high scores for accommodating, competing or avoiding, you may want to reflect on whether you too regularly:

- take decisions to please others, against your better judgement
- duck problems and avoid conflicts – anything for peace
- or have to have your own way at all costs

Sometimes it's more important to 'lose the battle to win the war'. If something matters a lot to someone else, but isn't crucial for you, do you still have to have it your way? Or are you ready to give in gracefully?

Co-laborate means to work with, remember.

Compromising is sometimes the best option you can arrive at, in a given situation. That means negotiating so that neither side gets all they seek, but both get something out of the situation.

Handling conflict

- If possible, be prepared for it. Keep your ear to the ground. Keep checking which way the land is lying. Know your team well, as individuals, and in respect of the team dynamics. Anticipate likely positions, objections and flashpoints. The good manager is rarely taken completely by surprise.

- Use breathing and body language to control your response.

  - **Breathing.** If conflict upsets you, focus on your breathing. That in itself will help to calm you. When stressed, we tend to breathe shallowly, from the top of the lungs. Focus on breathing from the abdomen. Take a deep breath, and then breathe out counting to ten. Focus on the out breath.

  - **Body language.** If you are getting tense, the likelihood is that you will be up-tight. That is UP: shoulders high, breathing from upper chest; and TIGHT: a great deal of tension in your upper body. Think DOWN. Feel your weight centring at the pelvis, to give you a solid, four-square feeling. Ground yourself: feet planted parallel on the floor, body straight (no crossed legs, or crossed arms). Tense then relax your hands, and the muscles in your upper body. Feel and hold that relaxation. Feel your authority.

- Use positive, assertive 'I' language.

  - **Keep your language positive**. Avoid negatives as far as you possibly can. Instead of: 'We can't outsource the mailout: it just won't work', what about 'That's an interesting idea; I'd like to explore how it would work: Can you give me any examples of similar organisations where you've seen it work well?' Use 'and', instead of 'but'.

  - **Assertive 'I' language.** Own your reservations, if you have them. Own responsibility for your own role and authority.

- **Be clear about your own position**. If necessary use the **broken record technique.** If you are clear about your bottom line, that's a great start. Find a phrase you can repeat, when the going gets tough. It will enable you to stand up for your position, and will let colleagues know you mean business. For example: 'we need to make sure the mailout happens on time', or whatever is a good 'anchor' for you.

Case study

Sandy is a new manager in a housing team. A new staff member, Justin, has been moved to her team from another project in the organisation. Justin has a history. He has regularly been moved around by the head office, every time problems have arisen.

Sandy's team has a motivated and 'together' attitude. They work well to give tenants in their project a good service. They already feel Justin is not pulling his weight. He spends time finding fault with everyone else's work, and not doing his own. Staff are finding this unsettling, and want Sandy to tackle it. Sandy feels harassed, and angry that previous managers and the head office seem to have passed the buck. How should she handle things?

Some options that Sandy could consider:

- Sandy has good reason to feel dumped on. She could consider going to her own manager to talk this difficult situation through. She could consider taking 'head office' on, but she would be wise to do so with support, if she can. There may be more to the situation than she understands.

- Maybe moving him to Sandy's project is a compliment: perhaps senior managers are confident Sandy is the best team leader to handle things.

- She, or somebody, does need to deal with the situation, or risk losing the loyalty and good will of the existing team members, all of whom will be looking to her to sort it out. Someone needs to take Justin on.

- If her own manager is supportive, Sandy may want to involve them in her session with Justin, if it turns out that she has to deal with things herself.

- If Justin is a long-serving member of staff there are likely to be records of supervision, and other meetings on file somewhere. Sandy needs to locate these. Have disciplinary procedures ever been invoked, for instance? Could there be a capability issue? Have any training and support needs been addressed, by previous managers? Has Justin been properly and appropriately managed? Sandy needs to arm herself with a full history.

- Sandy should start by treating Justin just as she would any other team member: offering him regular supervision sessions, asking him questions about how he is finding the work, the clients and the new team, listening carefully to his replies, planning workload, agreeing objectives, and agreeing action points as she would do with any other team member.

- She also needs to brush up on her organisation's policies and procedures. If she has, in the end, to resort to disciplinary measures, for example, she needs to be sure she is following organisational policy to the letter. It is always wise to look ahead to the worst-case scenario: perhaps Justin may take the organisation to court. Would Sandy's handling of things stand up?

- She must be sure to keep a paper trail. She will need to keep careful records of all agreements, commitments, and action points, on both sides, which are shared with Justin. If things get difficult, she may find it useful to write to him formally. Again, these records must be such that they will provide evidence that she has handled the matter fairly, reasonably and in accordance with employment law and the organisation's written policies, should the case ever come to court.

- Invoking the disciplinary procedure, which can lead eventually to dismissal, should be a last resort. Maybe the organisation has let Justin down in the past, rather than vice versa? Sandy will need to use every resource available to her to improve matters first. Terminating anybody's contract of employment is always a painful affair, though it may, sometimes, be the right thing.

- To dismiss an employee fairly, if it comes to that, takes time too. Whilst any process is going on, Sandy needs to be aware of potential difficulties around boundaries with the rest of the team. She should preserve confidentiality, whilst reassuring team members that action is being taken. If you have not been a manager, you don't always recognise that you can't 'just sack him'.

- Whatever proves to be the final outcome, Sandy will need support along the way. She should not feel she has to deal with this all by herself. She needs to know when she does not know, too: mistakes can be very costly. But it is important to seek support appropriately, and from the right people (i.e. not fellow team members).

- **Look for solutions which are WIN–WIN.** Strive for solutions which are **win–win**, in the familiar management phrase. Win–Win solutions ensure both sides get something they want and need. These contrast with the traditional Win–Lose outcomes, where I win, but at your expense (or vice versa).

- **If a fight breaks out – don't join in!** Never be afraid to take time out. Putting some distance between the warring parties is always a good objective. Consider 'parking' difficult issues, to come back to later. Suggest adjourning a difficult meeting for ten minutes, and/or taking a walk round the block. Stay neutral, as far as you can.

"THERE MUST BE A BETTER WAY
TO SORT THINGS OUT!"

7
Communication skills

How we communicate

In a famous experiment conducted by the psychologist Albert Mehrabian in the US, a group of people were studied to find out what they remembered, after a series of experiences of person-to-person interaction. The results were surprising. The researchers found that:

- 7–10% of what was recalled were the actual words used
- 30–35% was the tone of voice
- 50–55% was the body language

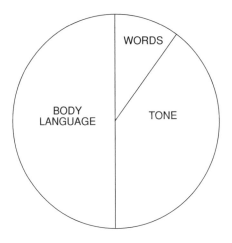

So the words count for far less, and the body language far more, than most of us imagine. In fact 'you cannot NOT communicate'.

Verbal and non-verbal

In face-to-face communication, your body language, and your tone of voice, will be crucial in the way your message is understood.

'Your body is never silent.'

What flows from this?

- That 'telling people things' is never that simple
- It's the way you deliver your message that counts; far more than you think. The medium really is the message (Marshall McLuhan).

An advert on the web stressing the importance of good communications says:

- 90% of problems in working life are people problems
- 90% of people problems are communication problems

You can begin to see why!

You and your tone

How well do you know your customary tone of voice? How do you feel about your voice on the answerphone, say? Most of us think: 'That can't be me!' But a good friend may be able to help here. Could it be that you come across to other people in a way that you have never intended? Do particular situations put 'an edge in your voice'? Or cause you to speak hesitantly, stridently, in a whisper or a bellow? It's well worth doing a few role play experiments, on audio or videotape. That helpful friend will be very useful here, for some frank but supportive feedback.

Tone-check. Is your tone of voice:

- Loud or soft?
- Warm or chilly?
- Curt or gentle?
- Varied or monotonous?
- Relaxed or edgy?

Your voice. Think about:

- Pitch
- Breathing

- Pace
- Clarity
- Projection

We are not talking about elocution lessons here, or about learning to speak so-called 'BBC English'. As long as you can be clearly understood, in the working context, a regional or cultural accent is valued by all organisations which pride themselves on fostering diversity in the workforce.

There is a good deal we can all learn, technically, about how the voice works. And we can all learn to project better, and to speak with more authority, if that's what's needed. Think about the difference a good voice coach has been known to make in the lives of actors, or politicians (Margaret Thatcher, or so we've been told) for example. Could you benefit from any help yourself?

Body language: what's important?

Most of us know the difference between so-called 'open' and 'closed' body language. Classic examples of closed body language are folded arms, and crossed legs – anything that makes you look defensive, and 'closed off'. Open body language is relaxed language.

But there is a whole repertoire of other things to consider, if we are to consider non-verbal cues and messages as a whole.

For instance:
- Posture and stance
- Eye contact and eye signals
- Facial expression
- Space and distance
- Use of hands: hands and arms, hands and face or hair
- Stillness as opposed to movement/fidgeting
- Gestures and mannerisms
- Meeting and greeting conventions
- Showing respect: cultural difference
- Territory and ownership

- Body position and status
- Space and furniture: chairs, tables and seating arrangements
- Dress and appearance

Aim for body language that conveys empathy and respect.

Body language: check:

- Eyes and eye contact?
- Face? smile (unless this gives mixed messages! You need to keep your words and facial expression **congruent**).
- Head: upright, confident?
- Arms and legs? (folded arms, crossed legs = 'closed')
- Hands? open gestures (no pointing fingers, not too much movement)
- Posture: centred or uncentred?
- Slouching or upright?
- Tense or relaxed?
- Leaning forward or backward (towards/away from)?
- Still or fidgety?
- Tapping feet/clinking change/twiddling rings/clicking pens?
- Mannerisms: have you watched yourself on video?
- Personal space: too close or too distant?
- Personal appearance: professional or sloppy?

But remember to filter this for cultural features, whether ethnic or organisational.

For example, in some cultures, direct eye contact is considered disrespectful (between genders, or age groups).

Similarly, in some organisations suits are expected, whilst in others, this would be quite inappropriate.

Matching and mirroring

When two people are in rapport, you will notice that their body language matches each other. This is instinctive, and intuitive. Notice people who seem to be in love, for example, or old friends talking together.

- If you seek to establish rapport with another, think about **matching** and **mirroring** their body language
- Do this subtly!
- Don't try it if they are angry or hostile. You may need to 'pace' things

Pacing and leading

If you seek to calm a difficult situation, here are a few suggestions:

- **Start at a similar level**, but 'down a gear'. If a hostile client is standing over you, it may help to stand up, to get 'on a level'. But take care that your gestures, tone and expression are not hostile too. You are endeavouring to 'pace' things, to 'talk the client down' towards a more rational position.
- **Pace, then lead**. You will know you are winning if you notice your client starting – even if slightly – to mirror you. E.g. you sit down, and then they sit down.

Consider your body language and tone in each of the following situations:

1. You are called to deal with an angry client in reception. He is shouting and standing over the receptionist in a threatening manner.

2. You have a one to one with a newish staff member. Her performance leaves something to be desired but you want to encourage her.

3. You are making a presentation at a conference. There is an audience of 100, most of whom you don't know.

4. You need to confront a colleague who has been bullying a member of your team.

5. You go to see your chief executive to discuss a promotion opportunity.

How would you aim to use your body to maximum effect, in these different situations?

What would you have to guard against?

The non-verbal aspects of communication have only been studied over the last few decades, though of course we have been giving each other non-verbal messages for far longer than we have been able to use language. It really helps to become aware of how your non-verbal messages are coming across. If you have not considered this before, get a friend to video you as you role play a difficult interview you are anticipating, or a presentation you have to make. You will learn a lot – more than you want, perhaps!

Case study

Robin has worked for many years in the same organisation. It has grown considerably during that time, and the management structure now means that he is working with three other managers at his level. He is finding it difficult to get on with one new manager in particular. He finds Sven abrupt, curt, impatient and uncooperative, although he acknowledges that Sven's work and his skills are of great value to the organisation.

He wants to deal with the situation, but finds it hard to say what he wants to say. Sven makes him feel anxious and ill at ease.

How can Robin increase his chances of communicating effectively with Sven?

Some options Robin could consider:

- Robin might benefit from working with someone else on this. Perhaps he has a mentor – either his manager, a colleague he knows and trusts, or someone independent of the organisation.

- He might find it useful to role play the scenario with Sven, and get a friend to video it for him.

- Practising the meeting with Sven might in itself be helpful, in clarifying his thoughts and honing his message. The video may be even more so – though it could be a bit painful. Perhaps Robin is dismayed to notice that he habitually smiles apologetically. Maybe he notices that he sways backwards and forwards whilst he is speaking, which his role-play partner describes as 'a bit distracting'. If he did not realise either of these things, it could be useful to learn that they are hampering communication.

- In discussion with his mentor, Robin may be able to work on both, to the benefit of his eventual meeting with Sven.

- Maybe Sven could do with a mentor and a bit of role play too – although this will be for him to discover!

Communicator, message, medium, receiver

In any written or spoken verbal transaction between people, there are four separate elements to be considered.

1. The communicator

One person or group conveys a message of some kind to another person or group.

Emotional intelligence

We hear a good deal today about emotional intelligence (EI), and emotional literacy. It is now believed that we all have an EQ as well as an IQ, for instance. One of the helpful insights from this field encourages us to think of the importance of standing back to consider our options before leaping into action, whether by dashing off an email or picking up the phone.

The 'amygdala hijack'

The theory behind this is that our emotional reactions are triggered by a more primitive part of the brain than our 'cognitive' ones – i.e. the reactions based on reason. EI theorists talk of the 'amygdala hijack': the amygdala is that part of the brain governing the emotions. Crucially, it works much faster than the cognitive bit: your 'primitive' responses will always come first.

Responses to threat: the three Fs

When our ancestors were threatened by sabre-toothed tigers, they had to react fast: no good considering options. The classic responses to threat are:

- Flight, or
- Fight

Modern EI theorists have add a third 'F'

- Freeze

Sabre-toothed tigers may no longer stalk the workplace, but aggressive colleagues, bullies, or clients who make us angry or upset can all trigger an unwelcome, and often unhelpful, emotional response.

It may help to think SOCS

When confronted with a task or an incident requiring a response, think

- *Situation*: what's happening here? What is REALLY going on?
- *Options*: how can I respond? Can I think of different ways I could handle things? Generating several options is good. Your 'default' response will be the primitive one
- *Consequences*: what are the likely results, in each case? For instance, is this something I can do by email or would a word in person be more effective? Would this be best put in writing?
- **Solution:** Having allowed time to consider, I will be able to select the most appropriate medium for this task

You will, with any luck, have averted the risk of the amygdala hijack.

It may help to think of a set of traffic lights.

Stop! Consider the **situation**	**RED**
Get ready! Consider **options** and their **consequences**	**AMBER**
Go! Select most appropriate **solution**	**GREEN**

(Adapted from *Emotional Intelligence* by Daniel Goleman, 1995)

2. The message

This is whatever the communicator wants to convey. For example it might be:

- An instruction
- Information

- A proposal or recommendation
- A request
- An invitation

There may be a more subtle aspect of any message. For example to convey:

- Approval
- Disapproval
- Attraction
- Dominance

Clarifying the message

Say you are a director thinking about the communication of revised guidelines for the induction of new staff, perhaps involving the introduction of a 'buddy' system for the first time. You need to communicate with section heads: they've all been consulted, but it has been left to you to draw up the guidelines. You have them ready to circulate, as an email attachment, and are drafting that all-important covering message. Here are some questions you can ask yourself, to test your plans:

- **What do you want to achieve?** Are you sure you have thought through exactly what outcome you seek? What exactly do you want your colleagues to do?
- **How will they take it?** Focus on your audience. Can you see benefits in the guidelines for those who are responsible for making them work? Stress these advantages. (More under **The Receiver** below.)
- **Are you convinced yourself** of the value of the guidelines you are communicating? Your enthusiasm, or lack of it, will come through in the way you express yourself.
- **Is there any interference?** Additional detail that doesn't need to be there? An emotional tone that isn't helpful? Edit out the '**interference**', the emotional static, the unnecessary detail.
- **Is your communication specific enough**? For instance:
  - **Is this a final draft, or the real thing?** Do you know whether you want comments on your proposals? Or is

there now no room for manoeuvre? (i.e. these are no longer proposals. In which case you are not requesting views, but advising of new procedures).

- **Is there a timescale you should specify?** And if so have you done so? Is it clear when colleagues will be expected to put these new procedures into effect? Or is it for immediate action? Will you review the operation of the new guidelines, and if so when?

- **Does this apply to everyone**, or are there exceptions?

- **Have you expressed yourself positively, neutrally or negatively?** Think positive! See if you can put any negative statements into a positive form. It makes a big difference to the energy, warmth and impact of your words.

- **How will you know you have succeeded?** What are your 'critical success factors'? It's always worth reminding yourself that, if the communication does not produce the results you want or expect, that is probably down to you, rather than your recipients. Back to the drawing board!

3. The medium

This is the means by which the communicator chooses to convey the message. Marshall McLuhan famously said: 'The medium *is* the message.'

It's vital to consider how you'll convey whatever it is you need to communicate. Is it sensitive, and concerning one individual? Then consider making time for a face-to-face meeting. Is it something factual that the whole team needs to know? Then consider a written message. All will then have the information they need – and will have a copy. Is it something formal, such as an invitation to a job interview? Then an old-fashioned letter is probably best. Are you making a request, or needing to know something fast, or dealing with a potentially tricky situation? Consider a phone call: it may be that you can do the job more effectively this way.

The crucial thing is to stop and consider your options before you act.

Email is probably the medium that has had most impact on office life in the recent past. Email was supposed to lead to the paperless office. But has it? Has it heck!

Some advantages of email are obvious:

- It's not as intrusive as the phone, or a 'chat'
- It's quick
- It provides an enduring record
- You can easily 'copy people in'
- It's cheaper than 'snail mail'
- Most of us can be self servicing
- You can send attachments

But email has some drawbacks:

- Volume can be overwhelming, in a busy office
- You can find yourself with even more paper, if you print off
- It can cut down too far on face-to-face communication
- It's easy to fire off an email which you later regret
- It's easy to send something to the wrong recipient
- You can get deluged with 'junk'
- Email has a 'demanding' feel to many, and disrupts concentration – especially if your computer bleeps at you when you have mail
- People may expect an instant response

Choosing your medium

What do you think would be the best way of communicating if you were tackling any of the following tasks?

1. Offering negative feedback to an individual staff member you manage

2. Setting up dates for a forthcoming senior management team meeting

3. Querying an invoice from a regular supplier

4. A request for an interview, to a high profile academic, to help you with some research you are doing

5. Letting the team know some good news about a major new grant

6. Consulting trustees on the new staff recruitment policy

It may help to think **PEP**

- Paper?
- Electronic?
- Personal?
  - Face to face? or
  - Phone?

You need to make a good choice of medium:

- The right **vehicle** for this job
- The right **slant** for this receiver/these receivers

4. The receiver

- The receiver is the most important link in this chain. No matter how clear you think your message is, you will have failed in your object if the receiver does not understand what you have meant to convey. It is tempting to blame 'them', but it may be more productive to look again at your own contribution. So you need to put yourself in your receiver's shoes
- The receiver needs to have the capacity to cope with your message: this might be a matter of ability, emotional state, or workload
- It's no good sending the right message but to the wrong person
- Seek first to understand and then to be understood
- Establish rapport!

Three insights from Neuro-Linguistic Programming (NLP) are helpful here:

- **The meaning of any communication is the effect it has.** This is one of the basic principles of NLP. It is a helpful reminder of the importance of putting yourself in the receiver's shoes. It's the outcomes that matter!

- **The map is not the territory. Every person's map is unique.** Another 'basic principle of excellence' from NLP, this reminds us that we all see the world differently. This may be blindingly obvious, but it is surprising how often we assume that other people at work will have the same priorities, preferences and interests as we do ourselves. Understanding 'where other people are coming from' is essential to good communications.

- **There is no failure, only feedback.** If you have not succeeded in getting your message across, have another look at the way you tried to do it. We are all familiar with the old adage 'If at first you don't succeed, try, try again'. NLP turns this old adage on its head and says: If at first you don't succeed, try something different!

Thomas Edison, when called a failure for having taken so long to invent the light bulb, responded: 'Every wrong attempt discarded is another step forward.'

Establishing rapport

'True rapport is the ability to dance in step with your partner.'

One to one: Most of the communication problems that cause us frustration and difficulty at work involve working with particular individuals. Does the case study overleaf ring any bells for you?

Are you on the same wavelength? Think VHF!

- Anyone who needs to achieve results through others needs to be able to connect with people

- You can't change someone else, only your own way of communicating with them

- One of the insights from NLP is that many of us have strong preferences for describing the world through one particular sense. The three main tendencies are:

Case study

You work with Peter, who is another manager on your level. He looks after the finances. You are a bit of a visionary, and new ideas are your speciality. But Peter has to agree to the funding. Often he says no. You try explaining the advantages of your new plans in different ways, to try to get him to see reason, but the more you try, the more he seems to be digging his heels in.

How can you improve communication between the two of you?

Some options you could consider:

- What's in it for Peter? If you have a difficult message to impart – say you're asking someone to agree to your proposals, or to change their working practice, or to take on more work, or to accept constructive criticism – try seeing what advantages or benefits there may be, for them, in your proposal. Stress these first.

- Try to think your way into Peter's shoes. What's he like? How does he like to work? How does he like material to be presented to him? Work from this perspective. You cannot change Peter: you can only change your own approach.

- At a guess, Peter is likely to be someone who does not like surprises. He's unlikely to agree to anything if he feels rushed, pressurised, or caught off guard. Are you giving him enough time to consider your plans? Are you presenting the level of detail he likes to see? Can you show the sort of logic he needs, to feel comfortable?

- Visual
- Hearing
- Feeling

How do you know which is your primary tendency? Describe how you chose your most recent holiday to a partner. Ask them to look out for whether you are using mainly:

- visual words and phrases; what you pictured, what you saw, what you read, and how clearly you could visualise it

- words and phrases about hearing – what your friends told you, what you'd heard, what it sounded like, or

- feeling words – 'It just felt like the sort of place I'd like'; 'I wanted somewhere to chill out'; 'I had good vibes about it'

When you are working on communicating well with someone else, listen for their own preferences, and use the words and phrases that will work for them.

"LET'S GET RID OF THE SCREEN AND
'PHONES AND TALK FACE TO FACE."

The 'like' principle

Another way in which you can develop rapport is to try to understand better how your 'receiver' sees the world: how they process information.

People like people who are like themselves.

We all have different 'maps'

If we don't stand back and reflect, we tend to assume that other people's 'maps' are the same as our own: that we will all see things the same way, and process information similarly. One of the most helpful lessons from NLP is to show us some of the ways in which we differ.

Modern research about the brain suggests that we all have unique ways of thinking and preferences for processing information.

Options and procedures

For example, some people want everything spelled out (the 'i's dotted and the 't's crossed) before they can feel comfortable with a new task. Others find this maddening: they want you to tell them the objective, and leave them to figure out how to achieve it. In NLP terms this is represented by the distinction between **options** (flexible: let me work it out for myself) and **procedures** (what are the rules?).

Other helpful pairs of opposites include:

- **Internal or external?** Are you completely self reliant and self determining, or do you depend on external approval for your sense of achievement?

- **General or specific?** Are you a 'big picture' person or do you need the detail sketched in before you can feel comfortable? Do you get bogged down in detail when you are explaining anything?

- **Proactive or reactive?** Are you the initiator, impatient to get things done, or do you prefer to react to the views and actions of others?

- **Sameness or difference?** Do you hate change, preferring to look for the common threads, to foster continuity? Or do you get a buzz from new experiences and feel restless without the stimulus of new ideas?

- **Towards or away from?** Are you an enthusiast, an optimist, deriving satisfaction from the achievement of your goals, even though you do not always spot the potential pitfalls? Or are you mistrustful of hopes and dreams, always ready to spot the snags in any plan, and a bit of a pessimist? Are you more likely to fight *against* something than *for* something?

Of course most of us are a mixture; neither one thing nor the other, but somewhere in between. Nevertheless, you may be interested to reflect on your own particular preferences, in so far as you know them (ask a critical friend!). And of course you will find it easier to spot tendencies in others.

Case study

Imogen is a 'procedures' person. She wants the figures in from all her team by the deadlines she has given, in order to allow time to complete the work on the monthly accounts on schedule. She has built in some contingency time, for unforeseen hitches with the accounts program. Nathan is an 'options focused' project manager with a country-wide brief. He is out of the office more often than he is in, and is forever missing Imogen's deadlines. He has suggested various ways round the situation, but Imogen will have none of it.

How can Imogen handle Nathan more effectively?

Some options Imogen could consider:

- Nathan probably thinks Imogen is a picky perfectionist with no imagination, and no ability to see how he is placed. She probably thinks Nathan is hopelessly slapdash and uncooperative, with no understanding of figures. Put like this, you can see what a wide communication gulf there is between them.

- Imogen needs to try to see the world through Nathan's eyes. How far can she accommodate to his needs, without losing sight of her own responsibilities? Can she talk through options that would work for both of them?

- Could she, for instance, agree with her own manager that Nathan has his own budget, and reports only every three months?

- Could she get her own manager involved in overseeing whatever arrangement they come up with, so that she doesn't have to do the chasing?

- Would Nathan recognise her generosity in coming up with a flexibility she probably finds difficult, and answer with a corresponding self discipline?

- The key is for Imogen to try to see the world according to Nathan's map, not just her own. It's hard!

If you find you are not getting anywhere in your attempts to communicate with a colleague, could it be that you really are at cross purposes? That you have such a different 'take' on things that you really do not seem to be looking at the same map?

Developing rapport means using language, and ways of seeing things, which will work for someone with a different map from yours. Start where they are, and you'll get a good deal further. Flexibility is a strength, not a weakness.

Setting

Just as tone and body language can influence communication non-verbally, so can the setting. Always ask yourself: if I have a choice, which is the most suitable setting for this interview/meeting?

Some things to think about:

- Public or private?
- My territory, or theirs, or somewhere neutral?
  - In the office, or away from the office?
- Interruptions: can they be avoided?
  - Have I switched my phone off?
- Refreshments? Offering a drink
- Furniture
  - 'Equal status' is best: similar types of seating
  - Layout: boardroom or coffee table?
  - Barriers? Am I hiding behind my desk?
  - Position? Avoid 'confrontational' or 'dominance' seating

Take care of the 'human needs' of your receiver(s), and set things up, as best you can, to show warmth, empathy and respect.

The essence of assertiveness

Assertiveness is about rights and responsibilities

When you are assertive you express your needs, opinions, feelings and ideas *and* you take responsibility for them.

Assertiveness is underpinned by a belief in yourself:

- that you are in control

- that you can change
- that you can learn
- that you can achieve

Assertive people recognise that other people have rights, too.

Case study

Katy has a supervision session planned with Anya, her new assistant. She books the meeting room, which has some comfy chairs and a coffee table at one end. She chooses this area for the meeting. She ensures that she and Anya sit at 'ten to three' angles to each other, in chairs of equal height and comfort, with the coffee table for their papers. She ensures privacy, and no interruptions (she is clear about time boundaries). She organises refreshments. She sits in a centred, attentive position, matching Anya's.

What else, if anything, should Katy consider?

Options for Katy:

- It seems to me that Katy has thought of most things! She has set her meeting up well, ensuring privacy, separate territory, 'matching' both furniture and body language.

- One final tip: it can be helpful, as a supervisor, to ensure you can see the clock from where you are, without turning. If you have booked a room without a clock, you may find it is less distracting to sit so that you can see your supervisee's watch: less distracting to glance at hers than at your own!

When you need assertive behaviour

What difficult situations do you experience that make you wish you were more assertive?

E.g. handling difficult customers, having to criticise someone's performance, giving presentations, being in the minority at a meeting, feeling angry about lack of cooperation.

What would be the assertive response if your boss asks you to work late and you have a pressing engagement?

What is assertive behaviour?

Assertive behaviour rests on four things:

1. Being clear about your needs, views, ideas and feelings

2. Taking responsibility for those needs etc. and for expressing those needs etc.

3. Recognising that everyone else also has needs, views, ideas and feelings

4. Standing up for your own needs, views, ideas and feelings in appropriate ways without ignoring, violating or denigrating the rights of another person

In other words, assertive people always aim for WIN–WIN situations.

What is aggressive behaviour?

Aggressive behaviour is very different from assertive behaviour. The aggressive person may be clear about their needs, views, ideas and feelings (although often they are not nearly as clear about them as they pretend) but they also:

- Think their needs etc. are more important than anyone else's

- Believe they contribute more than other people

- Ignore or dismiss the needs, views, ideas and feelings of other people

- Express their needs, views, ideas and feelings in inappropriate ways

They want a WIN for themselves, and they don't care about the cost to others.

What is indirect (passive aggressive) behaviour?

Indirect behaviour is really another form of aggressive behaviour. Indirect people get what they want by making everyone else feel guilty. They often hold themselves out as martyrs. But their behaviour, just like the aggressive person's, ignores the needs etc. of others and expresses their own needs in inappropriate ways. They are not being clear and straightforward; they are making everyone else responsible for how they feel.

The indirect person aims for a WIN for themselves. But if they don't win, they want the other person to feel bad about it, or unduly grateful (this will also be seen by the indirect person as a WIN).

What is passive behaviour?

Passive behaviour rests on four things:

1. Being unclear, unsure, unconfident or dishonest about your needs, views, ideas and feelings

2. Not taking responsibility for those needs etc. nor for expressing those needs etc.

3. Recognising that everyone else has needs, views, ideas and feelings – and thinking that their needs are more important than yours

4. Failing to express your needs etc. in appropriate ways

Passive people are trying to avoid conflict – even 'losing' is better than having conflict.

Passive behaviour is a problem for:

- you
- your colleagues
- your organisation

You

If you are passive...

- You put off unpleasant things (making a complaint, dealing with a difficult phone call etc.), but they have a habit of catching up with you, and may be worse when you come to deal with them
- At first you might feel proud at your tireless devotion and capacity for hard work – but this can soon turn to resentment

- You bottle up resentment at being 'put upon' – this can turn to stress (and, possibly, stress related illness, e.g. migraine, back ache, tiredness)
- Your personal PR will be less effective, so you may not get the promotion you deserve

Your colleagues

- Your colleagues may feel sorry for you at first, but, like the indirect person, you may also make them feel guilty
- There will be a lack of equality in your relationships with colleagues

Your organisation

- difficult situations are covered up
- difficult decisions are avoided
- the need for new initiatives and innovative new solutions may not be recognised

Confronting difficult situations assertively

It may help to think about a five point plan for dealing with a situation you want to change. Say you have a colleague who always comes late to meetings. You want to tackle the situation assertively. It may help to run through these steps as you prepare for the interview.

1. **Be specific**. Mention exactly what the situation is. Provide your evidence. (Is it one-off or regular?)

2. **State how you feel about the situation**. How you feel is how you feel. There is no arguing with this. If you honestly feel, on reflection, that you are overreacting, then it's useful to find out early: don't go on!

3. **Check out how the other person sees things**: ask open questions. 'Were you aware of that?'

4. **Be specific about what you want to change**. Seek solutions from the other person first, then offer practical suggestions. Again, check you are being reasonable, not 'picky'.

5. **Negotiate solutions.** Summarise the agreements. Aim for a win–win outcome if at all possible. Seek feedback.

A sample script

'When.........................happens'	give specific examples
' I have noticed that.......'	these are consequences
'I feel'	
'It seems like...................'	be specific
'It would help me if...........'	
'Next time......................'	
'Why don't we?'	offer solutions
'What if?'	
'How would you feel about that?'	seek feedback
'What are your views?'	

The four cornerstones of assertiveness

Watch out for:

- **Eye contact**. Make appropriate eye contact. This is likely to be a little more direct than in normal social interaction, but not so intense that it feels like staring. Be sure to recognise cultural difference.

- **Open body language.** Stay centred. Focus on a point in the middle of your body, an inch or so down from your navel, and halfway through. Plant your feet on the floor, as if they had roots like trees. Now relax, and bring your shoulders down. Avoid folding your arms in front of you or crossing your legs.

- **Even tone**. Keep your tone adult and matter-of-fact. Check that you don't harangue, cajole, whine or plead.

- **Non judgemental language**. Keep your language objective and factual. Avoid 'You always...' sentences. There is a metaphorical admonitory finger behind those, and the listener's hackles will rise.

Focus on the behaviour

Assertiveness requires assertive behaviour. We are all capable of it, though for some of us it requires practice. Focus on the behaviour, and the feelings of confidence and liberation should start to follow.

Listening skills

Good listening is another key communication skill. Active listening does far more to build relationships than many people realise. So how good a listener are you?

Most of us have our weaknesses as listeners, though few of us are aware of them. Which of these sounds like you?

Selective listening

- There are some individuals I avoid having to listen to
- There are some kinds of people I find difficult to listen to
- Some people's accent or tone make them scarcely worth listening to
- I 'tune out' on some topics
- I refuse to listen to things that make me feel uncomfortable
- I pay attention only to the good things I hear about me
- I pay attention only to the good things I hear about others
- I pay attention only to the bad things I hear about me
- I pay attention only to the bad things I hear about others
- I listen mainly for facts
- I listen mainly for feelings

Attention

- I let my mind wander and pursue my own thoughts
- I spend much of my time planning what I will say next
- I am easily distracted by things going on around me
- I have ways of kidding the speaker that I'm listening
- Sometimes my body language reveals that I'm bored, or irritated, or impatient

Interruptions

- I am always ready to jump in with my own ideas
- I interrupt if someone says something I disagree with
- I complete people's sentences for them
- I try to stop people if they are getting angry or upset
- If someone brings up a problem I tell them about something similar that happened to me

(Adapted from *The Manager's Book of Checklists*, by Derek Rowntree)

Tops tips for active listening

- Focus your attention on the speaker
- Demonstrate your attention by nodding and making encouraging sounds
- Demonstrate your empathy by respectful appropriate body language
- Check your eye contact: approximately 70–80% (in Western cultures) is about right. Too much is off-putting. Too little and it feels as though you're not interested
- Build rapport by appropriate matching and mirroring, in seating and posture
- Consider seating arrangements: try to sit at an angle, so that you can maintain appropriate eye contact without threatening (sitting opposite can feel confrontational)
- Don't interrupt, or finish people's sentences
- Check you have understood by asking questions for clarification
- Reflect back, without interpreting, to check understanding and to show you have listened carefully
- Ask open questions, to help people find their own solutions, when the time is right
- Summarise, from time to time, and at the end

8
Managing yourself

Managing yourself in role

The art of management often boils down to managing yourself in role. Responding appropriately, thinking clearly, making decisions, getting things done, engaging people: they all need a certain level of self awareness, and self discipline, In this last section we'll look at two closely related issues, stress management and time management.

Much has been written in recent years about stress management at work. Writers on the topic tend to divide into those who see structural (work based) issues as key, and those who focus on personal deficits (and coping strategies). In reality, they tend to go hand in hand.

Structural issues that can create stress at work include:

- Poor management
- Lack of clarity around job roles
- Restructuring and change
- Bullying and harassment from managers
- A blame culture
- Work overload
- Poor working conditions
- A long-hours culture

Personal issues that can create stress at work include:

- Life crises outside work
- Shyness and anxiety
- Perfectionism and control-freakery
- Poor social and interpersonal skills
- Poor time management
- Feeling indispensable

- Lack of assertiveness, and difficulty with boundaries
- Conflict with colleagues

We also know that work pressures affect different people very differently. What may stress me out completely, leaves you as cool as a cucumber. Some appear to thrive on adrenalin, whereas others run for cover at the first sign of a crisis. We all need to get to understand our pressure points, so that we can learn to manage them.

Whatever the cause, exposure to prolonged periods of stress is definitely bad for your health. The body suffers from excessive levels of the 'alert' chemicals, and symptoms such as alteration in sleep and eating patterns, a lowered resistance to infection, headaches or backaches, depression and panic attacks can follow. The system threatens to close down, routine jobs seem to take forever, your decision-making power disappears. When you get to 'burnout' stage, you can grind to a halt completely, and may need some weeks or months off work to recover.

So what to do? Here are some suggestions.

Tips for managing and reducing your stress

At work:

- set some priorities – make some realistic goals
- learn to say 'no'
- review how effectively you communicate, how you deal with conflict, manage others etc.
- organise your time effectively. If possible, build in some time each day when you can have no interruptions
- learn when and how to ask for help
- recognise your strengths and weaknesses
- accept short term stress instead of long term anxiety
- speak openly (and calmly) about your feelings when you feel angry or worried
- don't sit on problems – discuss them. Encourage others to do the same

General:

- develop your own understanding about stress (what causes you to feel stressed, how you react to it and how you can most effectively manage it)
- identify what you can change and what you can't. Learn to cope with what you can't
- recognise when pressure is building up. Watch for early warning signs of stress in yourself, your colleagues and family members
- listen to your body. Review how you treat it (eating, drinking, sleeping, exercise)
- review how you spend your time and energy at work and at home
- try hard to unwind once you get home – don't take work home. Learn how to relax – develop your own best way
- build in time for family, friends, sport and things you enjoy. Build in some 'me' time
- Use professional counselling services when things become overwhelming

Managing time

Managing your time wisely is another key skill for managers. Time, like money, can be spent wisely or foolishly. The first step is to know where yours goes. Keep a time diary for two or three days, Write down what you are doing every 15 minutes (if you can bear to). The results may surprise you. Did it shock you how long you spent browsing the web, or checking your emails, or chatting to colleagues about non-work topics? Did you become aware of the extent to which you are interrupted? Or how long it took you to get down to that report you'd been putting off starting?

The essential time management tools are:

- Prioritising tasks
- Planning and scheduling
- Organising
- Working together

Prioritising

Prioritising is one of the key skills to learn. It may help to start making the distinction between the urgent and the important in your in tray. Stephen Covey, author of *The Seven Habits of Highly Effective People* devised a grid to explore these differences (see figure below).

Urgent and important	Important and not urgent
Urgent and not important	Not urgent and not important

To work out what is **important**, for you, you need to have a clear sense of your job role and mission. You can't do everything. In what ways can you, uniquely, add value? What is the best use of your time? (Think what your time costs the organisation. That is sometimes salutary.)

The **urgent** tasks are those with a tight deadline: do it today! Or latest tomorrow!

Where everything in your in tray is **both urgent and important**, the result will be constant fire-fighting and crisis management. You will be at risk of burnout if you stay in this quadrant too long.

The key is to spend some time every day in the 'golden quadrant' (**Important and not urgent**), where the crucial development and relationship building parts of your job are likely to be.

The two lower quadrants are less vital. If it's **urgent but not important** (for you), should you be doing it? Is it the best use of your time?

If it's **neither urgent nor important**, then you really shouldn't go there! Free up your time for what really matters.

The top 15 time wasters

Here is a list of the worst thieves of time at work. Which of these apply to you? And how can you manage them more effectively?

- Constant telephone interruptions
- Indecision
- Meetings – too long and not really necessary!
- Switching priorities
- Lack of objectives
- Personal disorganisation – cluttered desk
- Ineffective delegation
- Butterflying from job to job – not finishing tasks
- Inadequate, inaccurate, delayed information or communication
- Socialising

- Office procedures not clearly established – confused line of responsibility or authority
- Constant, unnecessary checking up on others and their work
- Plunging into tasks without planning
- Lack of self discipline
- Allowing others to interrupt your work, e.g. solving their problems immediately

Good time management starts in the head, and not on paper or computer, but good systems, and good diary management really do help.

Some tips for managing your time more effectively

- **Mobilise the power of habit**. Get into the habit of planning at the same time each day, each week, each month, each quarter.
- **Write a to-do list**, whether on paper or electronically, always in the same place, and at the same time. Last thing (while you're still in work mode) is often best. (Clear your desk, so that you can see the wood!)
- **Use colour** to highlight similar tasks, or priorities. Use colour to help you wherever you can: it aids instant recognition and cheers you up.
- **Prioritise** your to-do list: A = High pay-off, B = Medium pay-off, C = Low pay-off. Make sure you do the As first.
- If you are faced with a difficult assignment **make a start**.
- Are you a lark or an owl? **Use your 'best' time of day** to get going.
- **Divide a big daunting project into manageable bite-sized chunks**. And make a start (again). You will feel much better once you've done so.
- **Find a quiet place to work**, if you have a job which needs concentration. Can you book time to work at home? Or is there a quiet office or meeting room you could use?

- **Intersperse the big tasks with the bitty ones.** Batch phone calls together. Once you're 'on a roll', even the harder calls get easier.

- **Manage your phone** proactively. Perhaps you can agree a rota for phone answering, or 'surgery times' for callers. Use voice mail and answerphones when you need to.

- **Manage interruptions** from colleagues proactively, without being abrupt. Encourage them to book a time, if their request in not urgent. If it is urgent, say 'I've got two minutes.' And stick to it!

- **Consider office policy on quiet time.** Some organisations have 'red time': that is time when no one answers their phones or chats, or interrupts each other for a given time each day, or week.

- **Develop office policy on emailing**: do you copy each other in to everything? Is it really necessary?

- **Develop office policy on archiving** (to give yourself license to throw more away!) Agree how long you will keep different classes of document.

- **Look ahead.** Don't agree to take on a new commitment if you can't see when you will do it. Familiarise yourself with key deadlines, and plan accordingly. If you need to renegotiate a deadline, do it early.

- Don't let your diary become a list of meetings with other people. **Book time ahead with yourself** to complete important pieces of work.

- **Consider your attendance at regular meetings.** Is it crucial for you to be at all of them? Have you got an important contribution to make? If not, can you negotiate your way out of any of them?

- **Organise your work station**, your in tray, your computer, your emails, your filing. Develop systems. Throw as much as you can away. Have regular 'purges' of paper. Office black bag days are a good idea.

- Use the **six Ds** approach with new paper; **Decide** (when each new task comes in) whether to **Dump** it (throw away/delete. Do this as much as you can. Clear the decks!), **Delegate** it (you can delegate upwards, and sideways as well as downwards), **Defer** (and **Diarise** it. OK so it's for you to do. But don't put it back in the in tray without telling yourself **when** you'll do it) **or Do** it. OK, just Do it!

- **Take breaks**: take lunch breaks, but also take regular time away from your computer. You will work more effectively if you do. Take holidays: make sure you take your full leave entitlement.
- **Take exercise**. This will energise you. Look after yourself.

Take care of yourself: you owe it to yourself and those who care about you.

Twelve top tips for managers

1. Learn how to listen. Genuine two way communication is vital

2. Recognise stress in yourself and others: too much can lead to burnout

3. Manage your time. It's a finite resource. Analyse how you spend it

4. Get organised. Get on top of the paperwork and the information overload

5. Leave work at work. Your briefcase is not a home for lost documents

6. Delegate. But remember the five anchors, and don't 'dump' or abdicate

7. If in doubt (a), ask. You can't know everything. People want you to succeed

8. If in doubt (b), sleep on it. Instant decisions are sometimes rash

9. Say thank you. Give positive strokes. Praise in public, criticise in private

10. Never stop planning. It's your job to think ahead

11. Learn from your mistakes. Celebrate success and learn from failure. 'A person who never made a mistake never made anything.'

12. Be true to yourself

I do hope this book has helped you to become an even more brilliant manager than you already are. It's a career-long journey. Good luck on yours.

Personal action plan

If you have enjoyed reading this book, it might be helpful to write down what you have learned about yourself and your management style, any areas you think you need to work on, and any action you plan to take. Research has shown that 66% of new learning disappears, if not put into practice within ten days.

> *'If you always do what you've always done, you'll always get what you've always got.'* (Anon)

So why not commit yourself to taking stock? If you set yourself something you can do, achieve, or change within a week, say, you will get a 'quick win', which will give you the motivation to carry on to the medium term goals, and then the longer term ones.

A. My strengths as a manager are:

    1.

    2.

    3.

    4.

B. Areas for development for me are:

    1.

    2.

    3.

    4.

C. I will take the following action by (add dates)

    1.   by

    2.   by

    3.   by

    4.   by

D. I can get support from

E. I will review progress by

Further reading: a selection

Adirondack, Sandy. *Just About Managing?*
Effective management for voluntary organisations and community groups. London Voluntary Service Council. Third edition 1998

Allcock, Debra. *High Flying*
The essential guide to your first management job and how to make a success of it. Industrial Society 1999

Berne, Eric. *Games People Play*
The classic introduction to transactional analysis. Penguin Books 1970

Burnell, John. *Managing People in Charities*
An overview of personnel management for the busy charity manager. ICSA Publishing Ltd Second edition 2001

Covey, Stephen. *The 7 Habits of Highly Effective People*
A popular management classic. Simon and Schuster 1989

Goleman, Daniel. *Emotional Intelligence*
An introduction to the EI revolution. Bloomsbury 1996

Handy, Charles. *Inside Organisations*
21 ideas for managers. BBC Books 1990

Hudson, Mike. *Managing Without Profit*
The art of managing third sector organisations. Penguin Books 1995

Jay, Ros. *Manager's Manual. Work at the Speed of Life*
A 'fast thinking' guide for the new manager. Pearson Education 2001

Lawrie, Alan. *The Complete Guide to Business and Strategic Planning*
A practical guide for charities. Directory of Social Change. Second edition 2001

Rowntree, Derek. *The Manager's Book of Checklists*
Instant management solutions when you need them. Prentice Hall. (Commissioned by the Institute of Management) 2000

Shapiro, Mo. *Understanding Neuro-Linguistic Programming in a Week*
A handy introduction to NLP. Institute of Management/Hodder and Stoughton 1998

Turner, David. *Liberating Leadership*
A manager's guide to the new leadership. Industrial Society 1998

Index

Compiled by Sue Carlton

About the author

Julia Braggins is the Centre for Strategy and Communication specialist on organisation management. She has developed many of the Centre's management and leadership training courses.

Before joining CSC she was Director of the Centre for Crime and Justice Studies. Her previous experience includes work as a tutor and counsellor for the Open University, a prison education tutor, and a manager in adult and community education.

Currently, as well as working at the Centre, she is a freelance researcher, a non-managerial supervisor and on the boards of two national charities.